# Advanced Praise For Playful Rebellion:
## Maximize Workplace Success Through The Power of Play

"As a corporate facilitator, I interact frequently with people who tragically believe the time in their life for play is long over. Work can be playful, people! If you don't want to get to the end of your life with regrets that you should have laughed more, played more, connected more joyfully with the people you love, pick up this book. Gary Ware gives you the blueprint for your own Playful Rebellion."
**- Pam Victor, Head of Happiness, Happier Valley Comedy**
**Author of Improvisation at the Speed of Life: The TJ and Dave Book**

"Playful Rebellion clearly explains how anyone can live a more creative and expansive life by being more playful, particularly at work. I learned so much from the prompts, assessments, and resources that Gary shares, and I feel powered up!"
**- Amy Lisewski, CEO & Co-Artistic Director, Finest City Improv Author of Relax, We're All Just Making This Stuff Up!: Using the tools of improvisation to cultivate more courage and joy in your life**

"Gary Ware's Playful Rebellion is a must-read for anyone who wants to recapture the joy of play in their adult life. Ware offers a wealth of insights and practical advice on how to make time for play, even when life is hectic and responsibilities are piling up. With humor and wisdom, Ware shows how play can help us cope with stress, connect with others and find meaning in our work. This is a book that will make you laugh, think and change the way you look at play."
**-Stephanie Liu, CEO of Captivate on Command, Co-Author of Ultimate Guide to Social Media Marketing**

As someone who studies work-life balance and productivity, Playful Rebellion provides an essential puzzle piece in solving the success equation. While it might at time seem counter-intuitive, play is absolutely needed to get more done! Gary eloquently explains how to do this in the most fun and efficient way, with steps on how to play that don't sacrifice success in the workplace.
**-Apryl Schlueter, Author of Finding Success in Balance: My Journey to The Cheerful Mind**

In a world of hyper-curated personal brands and corporate experts, it's liberating to read a book so down-to-earth from someone who deeply understands what they're talking about. Playful Rebellion is fun, inspiring, and practical because Gary embodies those very same things. It reads like a wise friend sitting across from you. One hand is sipping a cup of coffee. The other is handing you a lightsaber inviting you to the adventure your kid-self used to dream of
**- CJ Casciotta, Author of Get Weir**
**Art of Being Ordi**

D1453303

MAXIMIZE
WORKPLACE
SUCCESS

# PLAYFUL
# REBELLION

THROUGH THE
POWER OF PLAY

## GARY WARE

Illustrations by Sarah Moyle

Playful Rebellion: Maximize Workplace Success Through
The Power of Play
© Copyright 2022 Gary Ware

For more information, email gary@breakthroughplay.com.

Cover Design: Onur Aksoy (www.onegraphica.com)
Illustrations: Sarah Moyle (sarahmoyle.com)
Interior Design: Bex Olesek (itsbex.com)
Author Photo: Orlando Martinez
ISBN:      979-8-9861816-0-8 (paperback)
979-8-9861816-1-5 (ebook)
979-8-9861816-2-2 (audiobook)
Library of Congress Control Number: 2022908025

*To Garrett, Cameron, Aaliyah, Adalyn,
Darian, Sebastian, and Jonathan.*

*Thank you for inspiring me to play and
be playful. May you never lose
that childlike wonder and imagination.*

# TABLE OF CONTENTS

# DISCLAIMER

BY READING THIS BOOK AND ENGAGING IN ITS ACTIVITIES, YOUR LIFE MAY BECOME EXTRAORDINARY IN THE MOST UNEXPECTED WAYS!

# Introduction

Thank you for choosing Playful Rebellion: Maximize Workplace Success through the Power of Play.

The following chapters will discuss my methods of bringing playfulness to your life and workplace. I'll tell you why bringing a sense of playfulness back into your life is essential for your health and well-being, and tell you how to do so. In this book, you'll find a step-by-step guide to unleash your inner child and bring joy back into your life by nourishing your Playful Spirit.

There are plenty of books on this subject on the market; thanks again for choosing this one! Every effort was made to ensure it is full of as much useful information as possible; please have fun!

Before we get started, I'd like to invite you to join the community.

You can register at breakthroughplay.com/rebellion.
Once you are in the community you will get access to additional resources along with invitations to our various play challenges.

CHAPTER 1:
# WHY DON'T WE PLAY?

# CHAPTER 1: WHY DON'T WE PLAY?

**Play is the cheat code to business success, and leaders who are serious about leading need to cultivate play for themselves and their employees!**

When I was a young boy, my dad gave me some advice that worked until I became an adult; he said, "Gary, you can play when your work is done." That advice drove me from then on because I loved to play! I would race home from school every day to get my homework done. Then I would play. I would do anything and everything: playing video games, playing outside, sports. If I were playing, I was happy. That served me until I became an adult and had to go to work.

The interesting thing is, in every job that I started, I was very playful; I saw the work as play. But quickly after that, I would go from seeing the world as a playground to seeing the world as a proving ground. The work was never done. It was never time to play based on that old belief.

## The Mindset

The belief that play is the opposite of work and that you can only play when all your work is complete, tricks you into seeing the world as a proving ground. Businesses now insist their employees work many hours a week and regularly prove their abilities if they want to succeed or even stay employed! Members of the workforce are expected to follow the same road to success: get a good job, move up the corporate ladder, pay your dues, put in the hours, collect your retirement.

The list is the same for everyone—check, check, check.

These corporate mandates stem from the Protestant work ethic, which exemplifies work, sacrifice, and diligence. Part of the Protestant work ethic was the belief that if we were left to our own devices, we would get into trouble, stop working, and become degenerate, so the industrial age of work was all about command, control, and compliance. The factory owners gave the orders, and the masses of faceless workers obeyed. The average workweek was six days a week and twelve hours each day. Sundays were spent in church all day. The idea of play became nearly villainized, and people were working so hard that they were falling asleep on the job, causing accidents and safety issues. Workers were also spending less money on luxuries and leisure activities, causing profits to plummet in the automotive, tourism, and other industries. After all, who had time to go anywhere or do anything fun when they spent all their time working? So, Henry Ford became the first to challenge that status quo by campaigning for the forty-hour workweek.

People thought he was crazy, but then a funny (or should I say fun?) thing started to happen. People had enough time to play! Finally, with a limit to their hours spent at work, employees had the leisure time to enjoy being away from the workplace guilt-free. They even started spending money more freely on leisure products and activities (Like Henry's cars!). These methods worked for the type of tactical workforce that was common in Mr. Ford's era for decades. Workers were no longer dangerously exploited, and traditional motivators and deterrents like incentives, bonuses, pay reductions, and employment termination became less effective. Big businesses created a "new normal" for the workplace: a twenty-year career, climbing the corporate ladder, ending with retirement, and a pension.

## What Changed?

Before the Information Age, the only people we could reach at a moment's notice were doctors, drug dealers—and Mom, of course. Now, we can contact anyone in seconds. As a result, we have a constant bombardment of communications: emails, messages, phone calls, virtual meetings, etc. All this extra media decreases the amount of leisure/playtime and increases the workload that we take on, even when we aren't conscious of it. What we also don't realize is that it's all too much. We haven't stopped to rethink and ask ourselves, "Is there a better way?"

Corporate mandates deprive people of a sense of play because it's more efficient for them. Leaders don't realize that those mandates are going to hurt the employees in the long run as they are overworked, stressed, anxious, frustrated, demoralized, and feeling trapped in what was once considered "The American Dream." Creativity is at a low, and nobody has time to play. Our workforce, and especially the corporate workforce, have been conditioned to accept the "facts" that:

○ Play is only for when the work is done.
○ The opposite of work is play.
○ Play is a waste of time.
○ Play is only for kids.
○ As adults, it's normal to forget how to play.

When in reality:

○ We are wired for play.
○ Everyone at their core is creative.
○ The ability to see your work as play is a superpower.
○ Playful leaders are more persuasive.
○ The opposite of play is depression.
○ Play can connect teams, unlock creativity, reduce stress, and increase productivity.

"Big Business" has decided that Play is a frivolous and pointless activity and is trying to steer our workforce down the path of the Protestant work ethic again because that's what worked before. Contrary to the constant push for risk-taking and innovation, if you make a mistake on your job, you're penalized. That's going to keep you from playing because you don't want to get fired.

Comparison and competition also keep us from playing. If you constantly feel as though you need to be better than your peers, you're not going to play. Play is risky and messy, and it's about experimentation. If you must be perfect and your livelihood depends on you being better than the "other guy," you're not going to take risks, which means you're not playing. When you're not playing, you're not being true to yourself.

## The Game Is Rigged!

Henry Ford helped us transition from working twelve hours each day, six days every week, to just eight hours a day, five days per week, and everything worked out just fine! The new mindset was "If you love what you do, you'll never work a day in your life!" People could relax, and not worry about work so much.

Except, that never happened.

By that time, most people had already been conditioned to feel guilty if they weren't working or being productive. Humans are also naturally "wired" with a negativity bias. We see things as scarce and strive to hang on to them even when we're hurting ourselves. So, our workforce was left feeling guilty and under pressure to keep what they had, but unable to escape that trap. The playground once again became the proving ground, and employees continued to work themselves into exhaustion!

Unfortunately, today's labor market isn't much different. Research shows that employees who were overworked before the global pandemic of 2020 now work even longer hours from home despite not having a daily commute. We have even more technology, are more connected than we've ever been before, but we are experiencing record amounts of loneliness, depression, and burnout: all things that are not allowing us to be the best version of ourselves we can be!

People feel it's their duty to work hard, and they feel guilty if they don't. We tend to tie our self-worth up with our productivity. If we don't put in all those extra hours, when we aren't producing for our employers, we feel like we aren't as good as the people who do. It's a mindset that's been handed down and ingrained since people started working, and if left to our own devices, we'll work ourselves right into an early grave!

The real villain of this story is our social norms, our environments. They're outdated, the way that we are working is no longer working, and the only way out is rebellion. Deep down inside, we know the best way to connect, we know how to set up an environment that is going to be conducive to the way we need to work, but we're trapped, so it's time to break out!

Now, you may ask, "Gary, why is this important? Why should we fight for this?"

My answer is simple. We've been so busy making a living that many of us have forgotten what's even more important. Making a LIFE! On average, we spend about 35% of our time working. Do we really want to spend that much time being depressed, lonely, and stressed? Our programming has become out of date, and it's time for an upgrade!

Back when our ancestors had to fight off predators and the elements, if there was a stressor coming at us, our body would produce cortisol and adrenaline to help us either fight, flee, or freeze. The blood started pumping from our brain to our extremities so that we could fight off that stressor, our heart rate increased, and our senses sharpened. Once that stressor was gone, we were able to go back to normal.

Well, the stressors we have now aren't the same stressors that we had back then, and they don't go away! That email from the boss that's looming at the top of our inbox, that message that came in at 8:00 p.m. last night from a coworker, the growing to-do list, even that 24/7 news feed is causing us stress. And unless we rebel, those stresses are going to keep piling up as we continue to be blocked from our Playground and our Playful Spirit, as well as being the best person we can be. The sad fact is, if you were to die today from stress-related illness, your employer would fill your role by the end of the month no matter how much they cared for you. But your friends and family are going to miss you forever. To them, you can't be replaced; you're invaluable and unique, and no amount of work can give them back the joy, love, and fulfillment you bring into their life!

## My Story

I was always the kid that was the super goofy class clown. One of my favorite holidays growing up was April Fool's Day because I would get up early that morning and booby-trap the whole house. My sister always hated it, but I had so much fun! And that didn't stop at home. In school, I was always the one cracking jokes. I didn't do it to be malicious or rude, joking was just how I connected with people. Observing this way of relating to others and wanting to help me be successful life, my dad would tell me, "Gary, there's a time for goofing off, and there is a time for work and focus. When you're at school, you need to focus; you can play when the work is done." Growing up as a black man in the late 60s and 70s, Dad didn't always have the same opportunities as I had. He knew that education was important and wanted me to get the best one possible.

I remember in second or third grade, the teacher had us do some sort of assignment where we had to sit in our seats and be still to write. Now, to a kid with ADHD, sitting still is very challenging. I somehow convinced my classmates that it would be best to work together, so instead of sitting still and working solo, we started to collaborate.

Well, the teacher did not like that at all and thought I was being disrespectful and defiant. She called my parents, (my dad specifically) and I knew when I got home, I was going to "get it." Of course, when my parents came home, I ended up in hot water, which became an ongoing situation! That was one of many instances where I was "rebelling" against what I thought we should do simply because that behavior was more natural to me. That's when I began to understand that sometimes play would get me in trouble. What I didn't know until years later is that play can be a great motivator in a structured situation to do the tedious work!

I wasn't officially diagnosed with ADHD until my mid-twenties when it also came to light that I was dyslexic. In the 80s, especially early in the decade, diagnoses like ADHD weren't as mainstream as they are now, and people didn't understand how to deal with them. Most people at that time would tell me, "Hey, sit still." Even my mom would say, "Hey, Gary, sit down, do your homework."

Neither of my parents went to college, and they wanted their kids to be successful. So, they instilled hard work and discipline, but they weren't tyrants. My parents were some of the most liberal, easygoing parents a kid could have. As a matter of fact, all my friends wanted to come and hang out at our house! But when it came to doing your work in school, that was number one. And you'd better not goof off! I think most people growing up in my generation heard the same from their parents. And because I loved to play, that was good motivation.

Throughout college and early into my career, at any new job after I graduated, that playful kid in me would always start out. I always saw the situation as a playground of opportunities. I jumped in with that curiosity, optimism, and excitement to be doing the work. But over time, my dad's voice would echo through my head, "Gary, you can only play when the work is done."

My lens shifted from seeing the world as a playground of possibilities to seeing it as a proving ground. I was proving to myself that I was worthy, that I was good enough. I was also trying to prove to the people I was working for that I was good enough,

that I should be promoted and valued. And while I feel like that did help me in my career, I don't think it's the most effective way of working.

One of the good friends I met in college, Steven Alcala, worked with me at a cable company in Los Angeles. We had the most remedial job: digitizing commercials to be played on the air; it was very tedious. Steven and I were extremely playful and goofed around a lot; however, we got our work done! We were super-efficient, even though all the other departments considered us the goof-offs of the company. I think that made those of us in our workgroup a lot closer than many others at the company were, too.

As I moved up in my career, I found myself at a digital marketing agency. I was employee number twenty-three, and by the time I left about five years later, I was a senior director, and there were over two hundred employees worldwide; we grew fast! In the beginning, as employee number twenty-three, it started as play. We worked really hard with long hours; it was a very taxing job, but some of the things that we did were so much fun. Then, as the company grew, they said we needed to grow up too.

Fun had always been one of our company values, but as we grew into a more mature agency, leadership changed their value statement. I remember like it was yesterday; we had this big ceremony where they unveiled these new values. They were posted with these inspirational pictures all over the office. There came a day when they finally they took the "fun" value down and replaced it with things like "excellence." I didn't realize it was happening then, but that was when we started seeing the world as a proving ground. We still worked just as hard, but the burnout came faster.

That was one of the first times when I started to feel broken because I was still working just as hard, but I was tired all the time. The "Fun" was gone, but I just thought that was part of the job, and I started to see my work as my identity. I was trying to prove that I was worthy of my work. I wouldn't take vacations and would work long hours.

It wouldn't be until eight years later that I managed to connect with some of my mentors, one of which recommended that I take an improv class. When I first stepped foot into that improv class, the catalyst of play awoke and ignited my inner child. I got a taste of something that I had long forgotten—and I wanted more of it! The class was on a Monday, which were usually a super busy day at the agency handling reports and client demands, so I almost talked myself out of going… But I went anyway. There were fifteen other people there that were just like you and me, regular people. What ended up happening (the real magic!) was that I immersed myself in what I was doing for two hours.

It wouldn't be until eight years later that I managed to connect with some of my mentors, one of which recommended that I take an improv class. When I first stepped foot into that improv class, the catalyst of play awoke and ignited my inner child. I got a taste of something that I had long forgotten—and I wanted more of it! The class was on a Monday, which were usually a super busy day at the agency handling reports and client demands, so I almost talked myself out going… But I went anyway. There were fifteen other people there that were just like you and me, regular people. What ended up happening (the real magic!) was that I immersed myself in what I was doing for two hours.

I was totally present, playing these silly games designed to help people step on a stage and think on their feet. The class included collaboration and many other things. But I wasn't thinking of any of that. I wasn't thinking about the fact that I was there to get better at public speaking. I was laughing! I was playing, and we were all invested because it was fun.

Two hours went by like that. I was in a state of flow. I remember stepping out of that theater with fifteen brand-new friends, people that I didn't even know before then. We were strangers, but we learned how to listen better and communicate openly because we had this immersive experience where we could be vulnerable and make mistakes. We naturally got closer, and that was the magical part.

The Tuesday after that class was the best Tuesday I had had in a long time. The clients were still there, the work was still there, and there was still a lot of stuff I had to deal with, but I saw it differently for some reason. That following Sunday, when most people dread Monday because they have to go back to work, I was excited. "I get to do improv! I get to play!" That became my new form of Play and my new mantra. From there, I introduced that sense of fun to my team and coworkers because I instinctively saw the benefits and the changes in myself.

That's how I started on this journey. That is where I learned to Playfully Rebel.

In all honesty, my rediscovery of Play came out of desperation. I thought my job was to move up the ranks at a digital marketing agency and eventually own an agency. That opportunity did come. I joined an agency as a partner, and I thought, "We're gonna change the world; we're going to change the way that agencies run!" In the beginning, it was very playful, but then I started seeing that proving ground stress again. I was trying to get that work/life harmony where the work allowed me to do things that brought me joy.

This was also around the time when my son was born. When I was growing up, my dad worked a lot, and I didn't become close to him until I was a lot older. So, when my son Garrett was born, I pledged that "I will be there, and I want to be part of his life."

At the same time, I was taking people on Adventure/Play retreats. For my birthday one year, my close friend, Amy Angelilli, and I led this retreat in Nicaragua for six or seven of us. We were doing improv-related activities and fun stuff on the island, including a service project for a school. On the last day, I remember being on the beach, looking at the sunset, and saying to myself, "Wow, I have a good life. I'm able to do this stuff that I love, and I have a job that can support my family and me."

I guess the universe had different plans for me because when I got back that Monday, while I was checking in with my business partner, he said he thought we should go our separate ways. He even had a buy-out check for me. Suddenly, I was unemployed. To make matters worse, two hours after that meeting, our land-lord called to tell me and my wife that he had to sell our house. We had to move, my wife wasn't working, my son was just about a year old, and I had to figure out what to do next!

That's when I decided that I could get another job, but I would most likely be miserable. The cycle of seeing the world as a playground evolving into seeing the world as a proving ground would start all over. Thankfully, my wife gave me the support I needed by saying, "Gary, you're getting so much joy out of these things that you're doing. Why don't you try to do more of that?" That's when Breakthrough Play went from being a hobby to my primary mission in life.

The stumbling block that I kept hitting, though, was fighting the corporate mandates, the conditioning we've all been subjected to so the companies we work for can improve profits. I started doing workshops and noticed that when people were in the workshops, they would play. They had fun and engaged in the activities we did, and that was great! But guess what? After the oasis of the workshop ended, they went back to work... And because of their conditioning, the proving ground kept coming back.

## Time to Rebel!

Playing isn't just beneficial because of the emotional, chemical, and creative boosts it gives; play is essential for a person's well-being. The opposite of playing isn't working, it is depression, and depression often happens when someone suffers from play deprivation. These conditions lead to more severe concerns, including burnout, illness, and stagnation.

We need to rebel. We must rebel against the status quo, rebel against our "adult" selves, and relearn how to play! My mission is to help more companies and more individuals use the power of Play to help them become the best version of themselves possible!

REGRETS OF THE DYING

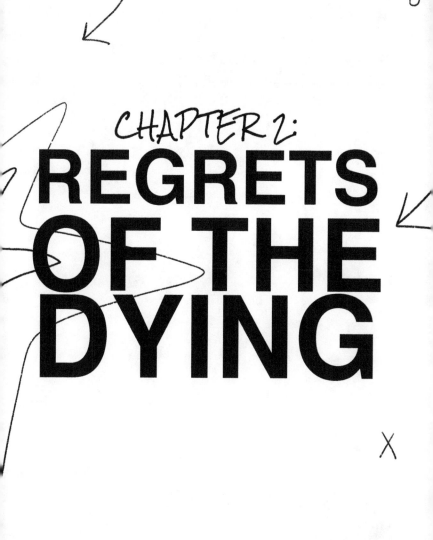

CHAPTER 2:
# REGRETS OF THE DYING

# CHAPTER 2: REGRETS OF THE DYING

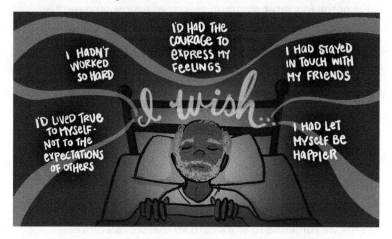

I was at the CORE Strength Experience with Michael Bernoff, a conference in Scottsdale, Arizona, back in 2015. I told myself I would improve my communication, get better at sales, interact with clients, etc. They started by asking the audience how many of us wanted to make more money, get more clients, be better at closing—all the lingo. Of course, many hands went up all around. Then they said, "Most of you, because of the way you're currently living, won't get those things." I was utterly taken aback. We were doing exactly what we were supposed to be doing, right?

That's when I learned about the Regrets of the Dying.

Bronnie Ware is a nurse working in palliative care who wrote a book about her time as a hospice nurse called The Top Five Regrets of the Dying: A Life Transformed by the Dearly Departing. She surveyed people in the last weeks of their life and comprised a list of the five most common regrets of people who were on their deathbeds. The first one was, "I wish I'd had the courage to live a life true to myself, not the life others expected of me." When I heard that, it hit home. But I thought, "That's what I'm supposed to do. Right?" Then I started to get angry.

"But isn't that what we're supposed to do?"

"Isn't that why we're here?"

"Aren't we supposed to work hard so that we can retire?"
But that's an old script. We've been conditioned to think that way ever since our friend Mr. Ford, proposed his forty-hour workweek.

Second, "I wish I hadn't worked so hard." In her book, Bronnie tells us that, although many women experience this regret, most of the people she was nursing were generally born before women joined the workforce in large numbers. The men, however, were a completely different story altogether! Bronnie goes on to say that every single male patient she nursed had this regret. What a wake-up call! Now more than ever, people are missing out on huge pieces of their own lives, their children's youth, and companivonship from partners because they're too busy working!

The third regret of the dying was "I wish I'd had the courage to express my feelings." When we don't express ourselves honestly and keep our true feelings bottled up and shut away, it only leads to resentment and bitterness towards those around us and ourselves. Nobody wants to experience the heartbreak of being alone on our deathbed because we couldn't share our feelings with others.

Fourth: "I wish I had stayed in touch with my friends." Later, I'll talk about making connections with the people around you and how important it is to build relationships. I feel that this ties into what Bronnie is talking about when she says, "Love and relationships are what matter most in the end." Letting friendships slip by, not making or keeping those connections, will rob a person of the comfort and love that only friends can offer.

Finally, the fifth regret is, "I wish that I had let myself be happier." It's important to note, here, that this regret speaks of letting yourself be happy. Being happy or joyful is a choice! Unfortunately, people will often choose the familiarity of old patterns and habits simply because it's more comfortable than breaking those patterns and allowing yourself to feel joy.

It made me think about a good friend of mine, Jhed, who was a mentee of mine. I met him right out of college, and he ended up working for me in multiple capacities. He was one of my best students and had such a bright future. He started stock trading and was trying to prioritize the important things in his life.

Finally, Jhed decided to travel the world. He took time off from work to live life at its best and had some amazing experiences. When he came back, he ended up getting a job, and doing great work to move forward in his career. Jhed wanted to do so much, and I was happy to be part of those things.

Then the unthinkable happened: he was diagnosed with cancer.

Again.

The diagnosis came nearly on the eve of his ten-year remission anniversary.

But Jhed made sure that he didn't have all those regrets. He knew what was most important and made time for it. Many of us don't. We don't know how much time we have left on this planet, and when you are on your deathbed, looking back, do you want to think about the time you spent being stressed out or following someone else's dream? I think about that all the time, and then I think about my own experience running my own agency. I went from seeing the world as a Playground to seeing it as a Proving Ground.

Most people think that the amount of effort they put into their work is equivalent to their value or worth. That's what keeps people working more than they should. I used to think to myself, "Well, you know, I'm having a hard time getting through all these tasks. Let me stay longer. I'll just put in a few extra hours." When that wasn't enough, I started to come in even earlier. I thought, "You know, maybe I just need to get in a few hours earlier and knock through this." I often joke that, at the time, I felt like my to-do list was reproducing whenever I looked away! Just like in the tribbles in Star Trek, it became an endless supply of things to do!

## Wake Up and Play!

The most significant wake-up call came for me late one night, on my commute home from work. After an extremely long workday, I desperately wanted to get home. The AC was blasting on my face in the car, the radio was all the way up, and I was crunching ice cubes to stay awake. I was doing everything I could to keep going even though I was exhausted. Suddenly, for a split second, I dozed off! I was so frightened that I had to pull over. My entire life could have ended very tragically, right then and there, just because I felt like I had to work more.

It made me think of what my life would be like in the end. What will people say at my funeral? Will they be talking about what a great guy Gary was? Will they say that he was always working, or will they talk about the good times? Will I have those five regrets on my deathbed? We don't know how much time we have on this planet, but we can think about what sort of mark we want to leave in this world. We can live our life with intention by tracing our path from our Playground to where we are now.

## Our Conditioning

There are other consequences of stifling that Inner Child and its need to play. A Gallup research study shows that a stunning 70% of workers in the United States show up for work not committed to doing the best job they possibly can. They're entirely disengaged from their work.

What's more, 52% of U.S. workers are literally sleepwalking through their day, and 18% act out their unhappiness! Many of those people probably work in jobs that they thought were their dream jobs, but they're not happy. That means, if you're a part of that 70%, a large percentage of your life is spent not being happy.

In any given week, most people work an average of forty hours. With 168 hours in a week, that's 23% of the week spent in a disengaged state. They're not even paying attention! For over one-fifth of their lives, those people are on autopilot. The National Bureau of Economic Research shows that people are now working upwards of four extra hours per week. I think four hours is a low estimation, but even that much was enough to cause the Bureau of Health to recognize "burnout" as a severe medical condition.

This upsurge in work-related burnout goes back once again to our friend Henry Ford. During his time, people could work forty hours each week and stop. They had a clear separation between work and play. Now, communication between coworkers is at a near-instantaneous level; the boundaries between work and play are beginning to blur.

Today, we injure ourselves simply by trying to keep up with technology! You see, we're still stuck in Mr. Ford's mentality of working hard until the job is done. Back in his day, the job stopped after forty hours. In the digital age, and with millions of people bringing their work into their homes because of the pandemic, working hard is beginning to mean working longer. We don't put in stopgaps and boundaries like we used to.

For example, I had this dog, Phyllis. Phyllis was such a happy-go-lucky dog with tons of energy. But Phyllis was the type of dog who also loved to eat! We had to give her measured amounts of food because if we just fed her the amount of food she's supposed to have each day at once, she would keep eating without stopping and eventually make herself sick. Good old Phyllis, she just didn't have a way of knowing when it was best to stop eating.

It's like work today. Back in the industrial age, there were clear starting and stopping points. The whistle or bell would sound, signaling that it was starting time, lunchtime, or time to go home. We no longer have these stopping points, and there's a lot of data that suggests that, just like Phyllis, we're not good at knowing when to stop. We don't know when to step away from our "work" bowls.

# Barriers to Play

Throughout the history of psychiatry, many prominent and knowledgeable people in the field have noted that human beings are "wired" for work. That's true. As individuals, we generally feel more fulfilled when we can contribute to our community. However, I think we're wired for play, too. Play is something that humans do naturally. A child doesn't need to be taught how to play; they just do. It's instinctive for us, like breathing.

Unfortunately, some conditions can make play challenging for us. When we won't (or don't know how to) step away from our "work" bowls, so to speak, we create natural barriers to playing and engaging in that playful spirit. We often get so caught up in our work that we don't even remember to or have time to play! These Barriers to Play are:

- Perfectionism
- Closed mindedness
- Extreme stress
- Exhaustion
- Comparison and Guilt
- Fear

We'll go more depth on these barriers later, but today's work environment contributes excessively to conditions that make play challenging for us by promoting these barriers as good working ethics. But humans are wired for playing! It's something that we need to do! We've been conditioned to work in a way that is no longer effective. The truth is, our conditioning is hurting us, causing illness and burnout. People often get conditioned to think this way because it's ingrained in our thought processes and work ethics, even from previous generations.

## Playful Rebellion

When we become overworked or stressed, cortisol and adrenaline begin coursing through our bodies. These two natural chemicals give us a quick energy boost in a short amount of time. The brain shuts off things like playfulness, which it doesn't deem necessary, to preserve energy to get out of the stressful situation.

Our immune systems also get compromised at these times, along with our ability to think creatively and feel joy. Working professionals in today's corporate setting are conditioned to work themselves to exhaustion and beyond! This mentality not only takes a toll on our drive and ability to play, but I've met too many remarkable people, professionals like myself, that are having their lives cut short from complications derived from this outdated work ethic.

We all know how important breathing is. If you hold your breath, you'll get lightheaded, dizzy; you collapse. Play deprivation causes issues almost as serious as not breathing; we become anxious and not as creative, we feel lonely and depressed, and our energy ebbs. The National Play Institute leader, Dr. Stuart Brown, said prolonged sustained play deprivation could have dire consequences on a person's well-being and competency.

Play deprivation could even have a link to violent, antisocial, criminal behavior. Adults that engage in insufficient play are also shown to be prone to economic inadequacy and long-term depression. In fact, Dr. Brown goes on to say that Play is a necessity for health, wellness, and complete expression of what it means to be human!

## Play Grows Your Brain!

Statistics show that creating a synapse in the brain takes about 400 repetitions of an action. However, by introducing play to the learning process, that number plummets to 20 repetitions! In a study on two groups of rats, one group could have playful interactions, and the second group was deprived of play.

When the researchers hid their food source under an obstacle, the rats who could play worked together as a group harder, were more optimistic, and eventually succeeded in finding their food source. But the rats who were play-deprived gave up. They weren't creative or socially developed enough to succeed in the task before the synapses in their brains were completed.

It's scary to think about, right? Too many people don't know the value of play and what it truly does for us! You see, I believe we get brainwashed to see playfulness in the wrong light. We undervalue it because we often see it as simply a frivolous and useless activity, but we do not know the asset it truly can be.

That's why we must rebel. We must break out of our conditioning and stop living in Henry Ford's workplace. And if we're going to rebel, well then, I say let's do it playfully!

THE PLAY REBELS

# CHAPTER 3:
# THE PLAY REBELS

# CHAPTER 3: THE PLAY REBELS

Back in 1991, Robin Williams and Dustin Hoffman starred in the movie Hook. As I watched, I remember thinking that Peter Pan, played by Williams, had a broken Compass of Joy. You see, I believe everyone has an internal guidance system called the Compass of Joy. It's an invaluable tool because it will always point you towards your Playground. Your Playground is a safe place where you can feel completely comfortable, let go of negativity, and play. It's the place where you can always find your joy.

In the movie, Peter Pan has grown up and become an adult. The problem is, he's completely forgotten who he once was. His name is now Peter Banning, and after becoming an adult, Peter forgets about his childhood and all the playfulness of being Pan. When he's thrust back into Neverland, he's completely forgotten that he can even feel joy. His inner child and playful spirit have atrophied, and he's not even capable of having fun anymore.

Too many adults today have this same problem. Perhaps not to the excessive levels of our hero, but their Playful Spirit has withered away, and they need help getting back to Neverland (their personal Playgrounds). Typically, people find their way to the Playground using their Compass of Joy, but when it needs to be "recalibrated," it's easy to get lost along the way and give up on play altogether.

So, what exactly is this Compass of Joy? As I said before, your Compass of Joy points to your Playground. It doesn't necessarily point to a geographic location; it points to the place where you find your joy. That may be a specific place, but it might also be an action, a person, or a dream. joy is something you can use as your guiding light to get you through tough times.

That's what separates joy from happiness. Happiness is often something that comes from outside you; it stays if the circumstances don't change. But Happiness is fleeting. Joy is different. Joy can be felt all the time, any time, even when you're not feeling "happy." Joy is an intrinsic emotion that we can use to pull ourselves through dark times and remains a part of us as long as we allow it to stay, just like Peter in Hook. He was "happy" when he took over a company or had some other success in his work, but had no Joy in his life.

When someone is focused too much on finding happiness instead of joy, that person is usually left unfulfilled. That's because Happiness is more of an external balm. Whether it's shopping, food, houses, cars, or drugs, the sort of happiness that comes from those things is a temporary solution. Sure, we may get a quick surge of adrenaline or dopamine that runs through our body, but that good feeling will wear off eventually, and it takes larger and more frequent "doses" of that activity to get that feeling. When we play, though, our brains create what can be called our intrinsic D.O.S.E.

D.O.S.E. is an acronym that stands for Dopamine, Oxytocin, Serotonin, and Endorphins. They are the neurochemicals that help us be creative, connect with other people, and trust others. They also give us a sense of belonging and increase our focus. When you focus on things that bring you joy, you create that D.O.S.E.

Most people in today's working world spend a lot of time and money on something that makes them happy for a short while because their Compass of Joy is broken. They have a hard time engaging in things that bring them a true sense of joy because their Compass is calibrated to lead them to someone else's

Playground—their Joy. We go to the gym or take those yoga classes, we practice our sales pitches to become successful and climb the corporate ladder because we've been told that's what will make us happy, but we're following someone else's Compass!

If you look at your calendar and go over all the things you do every day, what percentage of your schedule are things that bring you joy and fulfillment? Now, look at all the obligations—the things you do because you must. Most of us do more things because they need to be done, not because they bring us Joy. As adults, we tend to put things that bring us joy to the side to make room for things that need to be done. This action gets repeated over and over until our Compass of Joy no longer points to our Playground; it points to someone else's. Hook showed us this when Wendy noted that Peter had become a pirate. Wendy may as well have come right out and told Peter his Compass was pointing the wrong way!

In the movie, Tinkerbell brought Peter back to Neverland, and Rufio with his Lost Boys taught him how to "Fight, fly, and crow." They were helping Peter recalibrate his Compass of Joy. In fact, if some of the things I've been talking about so far have been sounding a little too familiar, consider yourself Peter; I hope you'll allow me to be your Rufio and show you the way back to your playground!

# Following Your Compass of Joy

The benefits of play align with all the things that we need in our lives to thrive. Playing opens you up to the thrill of uncertainty by helping you to see obstacles and things in your way as an open challenge to grow. It also lets you see people you're playing with as playmates and collaborators rather than competition or adversaries. Our brains grow when we play, and we become better as human beings.

- We get more creative, and we're able to adapt and be more resilient. On top of that, it's enjoyable!
- We get our intrinsic D.O.S.E. of neurochemicals that our bodies need.
- Research shows that teams and groups that goof around and play with each other are more productive and have a higher level of trust for each other.

But it's easier said than done. Our conditioning will often cause us to go back into something called homeostasis immediately. According to the Encyclopedia of Britannica, homeostasis is any self-regulating process by which biological systems maintain stability while adjusting to optimal conditions for survival. In simpler terms, this means people tend to fall back on "what feels normal" even if that "normal" is unhealthy or negative. It's more comfortable, so we want to return to that.

In my workshops, I invite people to cross their arms, and I say, "Now look which one is on top and which one is on the bottom." Once they notice, I say, "All right, cool. Now uncross your arms and cross them in the opposite direction. Now, how does that feel?" Most people say, "Awkward," while many of them are still trying to figure out how to cross their arms the "wrong" way! But that awkwardness that you may feel when you start to incorporate play and want to go back to your usual way of being—homeostasis—is only temporary.

A Play Rebel uses rebellious actions to fight their conditioning and return to their playground. Those rebellious actions are small little habits that, when practiced over time, can start to feel more comfortable with that "opposite" way of being—that playful way of being. These actions will begin to become your new conditioning because you're recalibrating your Compass of Joy, and getting to your playground will become your new normal!

## The Playful Spirit

I also call your playful spirit a play drive, and it's just like a muscle. If you haven't used it in years, it will atrophy. To many adults suffering from the workplace conditioning of the corporate world, it may feel a little bit painful and awkward to try and play. But don't worry, with a little bit of practice, you can recalibrate your Compass of Joy so that you can use play for what it's worth—as a tool to help you be the best version of yourself you possibly can be.

It's ok to be a little scared, too; it's all good. That's a normal part of the process. Letting go of issues is a huge deal, and it's frightening. Fear is one of the Barriers to Play that I'll help you to conquer later. Most adults realigning their Compass of Joy also want to over-prepare for play. They feel the need to be correct, the uncertainty that they're not cut out for this, that they're not prepared. But those are Barriers that I'll help you cross in another chapter. Trust me, your own Peter Pan is in you, waiting to play!

## The Play Rebel

If you rebel against your conditioning just a little bit, it can start to change the way you see the world and your behavior over time. These are the Playful Virtues and Rebellious actions of a Play Rebel:

- O Commit to joy
- O Find the fun in a mundane task.
- O Do something that brings me joy.
- O Activating power-ups
- O Power up/down before/after a task.
- O Celebrate tiny wins.

O Radical acceptance of reality.

O Reframe a failure.

O Seek out invitations to play.

O Create a moment of connection with someone.

## Commit to Joy

Now that you know what your compass is supposed to point to, it's time to start searching actively! The way to get back on the path to the playground is by bringing joy back into your life. To do that, we need to think back to a time in our lives when we felt joy naturally: our youth. What were the things that you did when you were younger just for fun? Think about activities that could keep you occupied for hours when everything else seemed to melt away. Are you doing any of them now? I'm not a betting man, but I think that you probably aren't. Just spending a little bit of time thinking about what used to bring you joy can kindle a fire you may have thought extinguished forever: joy!

## Creativity

Play Rebels seek out opportunities to be creative. What activities in your past and present help to bring out that Playful Spirit in you? Start to think about things that increase your energy and find opportunities to bring more of those things and activities into your daily schedule. Being creative comes naturally during play, and the more you "practice" being creative by playing, the easier it will become.

## Curiosity and Wonder

Curiosity and Wonder are two best friends of a Play Rebel. Our work may be serious, but we don't have to take ourselves so seriously! One thing I do is keep an emergency clown nose; if I'm getting too serious, I put it on and giggle just by looking at myself. So, what are those things that are going to help you smile, help you laugh? Everywhere you go, try to think about how you can make it easy to be in that play-like state? An exercise to help bring out the sense of wonder and curiosity in yourself is to take a few minutes each day and make a list of five things that amazed, intrigued, or brought out that sense of wonder in you.

As adults, we get too caught up in what it's like to be an adult. But there's freedom in being silly or acting "inane." When you're silly, you take risks, and you're very playful and curious. Dogs are the perfect example. We may say they're not bright for running right through the mud, but the joy they get from it far exceeds any we would if we had to slog through a mud puddle.

See, dogs don't stop to think about getting muddy or what people will think about them, and they don't mind the risks of getting in trouble. They're curious about what's on the other side of that mud, and they're always sure it's a treasure! Even when the "treasure" is just a muddy stick, the dog is thrilled to have found anything at all.

Dogs often exhibit this childlike behavior. People can too. But knowing the difference between childlike and childish behavior is what separates a Play Rebel from the conditioned masses. Child-like behavior includes the things we've been talking about: curiosity, wonder, joy, and even empathy. Childish behavior is acting selfish, throwing tantrums, or being spoiled. Childish behavior includes nothing of joy and will only atrophy the Playful Spirit.

## Find the Fun

As play rebels, it's our job to find the fun in everything. That includes even the mundane and boring or irritating things. I call this the Mary Poppins effect. You know, in Mary Poppins, the nanny says, "In every job that must be done, there is an element of fun. You find the fun and snap; the job's a game." As adults, yes, there are things that we must do that we don't like. Often, we feel like we just have to get through it because it has to be done, but when you look for even small bits of fun, that task will feel less like work and more like play.

## Create a Playful Environment

The places we spend time in are huge influences on our psyche and Play Drive. It's important to create an environment where fun can take place. I love dots of color, and I heard once in a TED Talk by Ingrid Fetell Lee titled "Where Joy Hides and How to Find It" that circles are the most joyous shapes out there. And I really took it to heart. I found these vinyl stickers on Amazon and stuck them all over the wall opposite my keyboard so I could always see them.

At first, because of the pandemic, I spent a lot of time in my office. I wanted to create a playful environment, so the dots were just where I could see them. It made a huge difference! Those little circle stickers really brought me joy. Next, I said to myself, "What if I can help bring other people joy?" So, then the dots started spreading, and now they're pretty much entirely across my office! I get positive comments all the time, and I believe they spread a little joy whenever someone sees them.

## Marvel at the Magic

So, what are the things that bring you joy? Ask yourself, how can you sprinkle them throughout your life? What can you do to see the magic all around you? One of the things that I love to do is called Brave Bots. These are little dominoes that are painted into these nifty little robots. Brave and joy bots are designed to give you the ability to be joyous at any moment; they look over you.

They can help you be brave or lift your spirits. These bots get left in random spots for people to find at odd times or places, and I love leaving them around the office. But rather than confine it just to work, I went to a park close to our house and left them there with a little note to explain what they were. Now, they come and go. They'll be there one day, and the next, be gone. Later, they come back, and it's so cool to see that people started playing the game. Recently, someone started putting inspirational quotes in chalk on the pavement too. The joy is spreading, and the magic is marvelous!

## Find the Fun in Mundane Tasks

There are things that we have to do that aren't always going to be fun. For example, one of the things that I really hate doing is invoices and logistical-type stuff. It's just not my cup of tea. But I have to do it. So, when I find myself having to do invoicing, instead of procrastinating and dreading the task until it builds up into a huge chore, what I do is say, "Alright, I'm going to step into this with my whole playful self. I'm going to set a timer for ten minutes, and I'm going to do as many invoices as I can in ten minutes. I put on my fun power-up playlist and get to work.

My son is also a master of this step. One of his weekly tasks is to pick up after the dogs in the backyard, but unlike most people that would dread the task, my son can't wait to get started. His secret is that he finds the fun in this mundane chore. He loves searching out and finding things. It's one of his favorite games, so he uses the task as an opportunity to play! He has a ton of fun every week making sure he finds every single "target!"

Do Something that Brings You Joy

The point to all of this is to find what brings you joy and incorporate more of it into your life. Play Rebels know that joy and wonder are everywhere, and we can make magic all around us! When we spend time doing something we love, we find ourselves feeling whole again. The playful spirit will start to revive, and our compass can lead us to our playground. But where do we start? How do we know what will make us happy and bring us the joy we've been missing? Simple.

We go time-traveling!

# The Play History

Dr. Stuart Brown, in his book on Play, talks about taking a play history. A Play History is simply a list of things that you did while you played. It's important to reflect on those activities because they brought us Joy, and that's what we want to recapture. Once we know what those things are and have a list of them, we can use that list to experiment and recalibrate our Compass of Joy. It's a simple process; think back, preferably to a time before you were twelve. Sometime around puberty, our brains go through a phase of getting rid of things that may not be needed after entering adulthood. The things we did while playing are often part of what gets tossed out, but the things we did right before puberty are often the best examples of what brought us joy. So, think of the things that you did when you were younger. What activities did you do just for sheer enjoyment? What were some of the things you did, sometimes for hours, when it felt like time just stood still? Those things that brought you so much joy that you would just do again, and again, and again.

Now, make a list of those things. I want you to think less about what those things were; don't worry about why you did them. Just concentrate on the feeling of joy they brought you. We're playing detective here and trying to go back and pick up the clues so that we can recalibrate our Compass of Joy. Your list will be a very personal thing. Play is unique to everyone, so no two lists are alike. But the main thing here is to keep it simple.

If you enjoyed Legos as a kid, borrow some from a kid you know. Don't worry about trying to duplicate your childhood, just focus on the play itself. Find one thing and make some space for it on your calendar and just see how it feels.

While you were daydreaming about your past, you probably felt surprisingly good. Now, sort of take a body scan. How do you feel now? While you were thinking about those activities and writing them down, you probably felt pleasant and nostalgic. If you got a little lost in daydreaming, GOOD! Even the simple act of thinking about having fun can help you rejuvenate.

Once you have your list, start to think about experimentation. Playfulness is inherently an experiment because it's messy and unstructured. Risk-taking is natural during play, and not everything works, but we have fun in the trying. Try an experiment: pick one of those things that you did and block out some time for it.

You might have to get creative; building forts is not as easy for an adult as for kids. But the essence of this exercise is to incorporate that activity in some way, shape, or form in your life. Maybe you need to build a couch fort instead of a treehouse, but why not? Perhaps even host your next Zoom meeting from your fort! Once again, it's not about the outcome; we're interested in the process. When I was younger, my dad and I used to build things all the time. I remember, one Christmas, he got me this Lego tank set. Hundreds and hundreds of parts to create this tank, and I had so much fun putting it all together. So, I bought a bunch of Legos on Amazon. Then I just started building stuff.

Some of the things I made followed instructions, and I got a feeling of satisfaction when I finished. I got a hit of dopamine, and it started to recalibrate my Compass of Joy. Other times, I just set a timer for ten minutes and built whatever came to mind. I get the same results either way because I'm having FUN! The process of doing it far outweighs the actual outcome.

## Conduct a Play History

Ok, Rebel, time to Play! Now that you know how to take a Play History. I'd like you to conduct one for yourself and then make a Playlist from it. Make an appointment in your schedule this week and go for it. Let yourself daydream about the fun times you had playing as a child and write them down. Just write the things you remember bringing you the most joy when you were a kid. Make your list and start to remember how much fun you used to have. Congratulations, you've just created a playlist by conducting a Play History! Woohoo! Pat yourself on the back, maybe even do a victory dance!

What a playlist does for you is to reduce your decisions. Highly successful professional people like Barack Obama or Mark Zuckerberg reduce the decisions they need to make. It helps them stay efficient. That's why Barack Obama only keeps two or three options for suits. He doesn't have to take the time to mull over a decision. I wanted to adapt that to play. So, I started creating playlists, and now I don't have to decide much when I'm in a situation where I need to be playful. I just refer to my list.

## Bonus Mission

Now, choose one activity from your Playlist that brought you joy and try it out again. Try to recreate some of that magic in your life now.

When I see you in the next chapter, Rebel, I'll help you find out what your Play Personalities are, and how to identify your Play Personality. Your Play Personality can help you choose the best types of play to use for your personal needs. It helps to eliminate the indecision of what kind of play to use when directing your playful energy.

ACTIVATING
POWER-UPS/
CELEBRATIONS

# CHAPTER 4:
# ACTIVATING POWER UPS/ CELEBRATIONS

# CHAPTER 4: ACTIVATING POWER UPS/ CELEBRATIONS

Energy is everywhere. It's in your body language, the way we speak, the people around us, and our environment. If you step into something with low energy, it is transmitted into everything you do. So, if we want to be the best version of ourselves and step into our work and play wholeheartedly, we need to acknowledge that it's essential to create an environment where we can be the best version of ourselves. It's also important to recognize how we're currently feeling. We've all been in those meetings, the ones where you may come in with the best intentions and one "Donnie Downer" steps in, and suddenly, they bring everything to an agonizing grind. So, you need to acknowledge where your energy level is during those times.

I learned the concept of "Energy is everything; everything's energy" from my mentor, Dave Buck, the man from whom I got my coaching certification. He introduced me to the idea that life is performance art. So, if you can take that same energy you would use during play and transmit it into the things you do, just like improvisational comedy, it just makes everything better. In this chapter, we're going to discuss the different ways to control our energy so we can become better Play Rebels and create a Playground wherever we go.

## Activating Power Ups/Power Downs

Because energy is everything, and everything is energy, we need to know what energetic state we need to be in for the task at hand. Do we need to be creative? Do we need to be focused or alert? We also need to know how to get into that mental state. For instance, celebrities like Michael Jordan or Barack Obama don't just jump into whatever they're doing; they warm up, rehearse, get ready. But we're professionals too, and we don't warm up our instrument—our brain! We don't often take time to get in the right state of mind. \

For instance, the first meeting of the day is important. That's the first time you're really talking to colleagues or bosses. Jumping right into that meeting as soon as you get out of bed doesn't seem like an intelligent thing to do, but many of us do exactly that for our first Zoom. However, just like Michael Jordan, you need to warm yourself up.

To do that, I tell people about a game that I learned from my friend, Anthony Veneziale. Using improv principles, he taught me a warmup called Boots and Cuts. Essentially, we're beatboxing, and it's hilariously silly. You exaggerate the pronunciation of "boots and cuts" and repeat the phrase over and over. In the process of doing that, you're warming and powering up your voice, so when you step into that meeting, you're in the right frame of mind, and you're ready to go. You're also having fun because it's a silly little exercise—it's play!

Powering Down is just as important after a task. Let's go back to our morning meeting. We powered up before going in by stimulating our creative energies and communication skills, but afterward, we need to power down or risk getting burnt out. It's like turning off the water faucet to save on your utility bill. Powering down helps us conserve our energy for a later time, so we use it more efficiently. Instead of jumping right into more work after that meeting, perhaps use a small, five-minute break to power yourself down by doing a crossword or playing a video game.

# Energy Is Everything, and Everything Is Energy

This concept always reminds me of my mom. She makes the most amazing mac and cheese. I mean, people love going to her house to get some of that mac and cheese! It's just so good! I asked her once when I was away at college to help me. I wanted to make this mac and cheese because my friends didn't believe how amazing it was.

Well, I found out that she didn't have a set recipe. She didn't use a "quarter-cup of milk," for example. Instead, she said she used "some" milk, "some" cheddar cheese, and "some" Velveeta. She walked me through it while I made it, but when I tasted it after finishing it, yuck! It was nothing like my mom's.

When I went back home, I watched my mom when she made it to find out what I had missed. It was her love! She was in this great mood, singing and finding joy in every step. I feel like that stuff is transmitted into her food somehow. No wonder it tastes so good! When people talk about pouring Love into the dish or Love being their secret ingredient, it's there; you can taste it!

You can transfer this concept to your everyday life, too. When you pour your positive energy into something and search for the joy in the tasks you do, you'll find that your results will improve exponentially. The more fun you have doing something, the more you'll want to continue and even improve. Of course, some of our tasks are not as fun as others—not many people love doing the dishes! But when we can enjoy ourselves regardless of what we're doing, we gain the advantage of having a positive experience instead of a negative one that will lead us further from our Playground. If it takes making a bubble sculpture in the dishwater, that's perfectly fine!

# Rest

Rest is essential for us Play Rebels because we need to make sure we have the energy to play. What's challenging about getting rest is that there's just so much that can be done! Research plus experience shows we're not great judges of whether we have enough rest to be effective and creative. That's one reason why we work so much. We think, "Oh, I'll be fine, I just need to push through instead of taking a break," When in reality, we need to energize ourselves to be more productive. Remember Phyllis, who didn't know when to step away from her bowl? Just like her, we need to rebel against the conditioning that has trained us not to step away from our "work bowls!"

It's all about working smarter, Rebels, not harder or longer! It's funny; we don't usually let our phones' batteries go all the way to zero charge and shut off. When they get close to dying, we panic.

We say, "Oh no! I gotta charge my battery; it's drained!" We'll go out of our way to make sure we charge our phones. But with our bodies, we often don't take the same precautions.

There are three different types of rest:

### 1. Macro Breaks

These breaks give you the space to allow your body to rest and rejuvenate, like sleeping. Sleep is vital; if we don't get proper rest, we won't see the world as a playground because our brain lacks the appropriate D.O.S.E. to keep our compass aligned.

### 2. Micro Breaks

Micro breaks are when you step away from your work and do something else. For example, when you take a lunch break and go outside your office, you're taking a micro break. Briefly stepping away from our work allows us to refresh, rejuvenate and adjust our energy levels for our next task. If we don't step away from our work once in a while, we become more susceptible to burnout.

## 3.  **Mezzo Breaks**

Mezzos are periods when you step away from work entirely, like a vacation. These breaks give your brain time to rebuild stores of energy and rejuvenate the Playful Spirit.

# Transitions

The pandemic is an excellent example of how important it is to use energy transitions. Most of us went from commuting to office buildings and working in cubicles to working at home. Most of us also thought we'd be more effective because we wouldn't have that commute anymore. So, we rolled out of bed and into work, and we found that we were working more! Now, we're more burnt out than we ever have been before.

Microsoft did a study on some of their employees where they looked at EKG readings from their home-workers and tracked them from meeting to meeting throughout their day. The ones who didn't transition or have breaks between meetings were utterly burned out and stressed by their fourth meeting. But the ones who took a small break after every meeting remained alert and fresh.

When people worldwide started working from home, they took the commute out of their daily routines. Very few people realized that our commute to work helped us be efficient. We didn't know how healthy that drive was for us. Because in that time, we could transition from home life to work life. It allowed us to get in the right headspace.

Remember when Mr. Rogers would come onto the set of his show singing the song, "Won't You Be My Neighbor?" He always came in, took off his jacket, and put on his cardigan. Then, he took off his outdoor shoes and put on his indoor ones. He was transitioning so that he could be in that completely present state of mind. And as adult kids, we operate the same way.

My son always needs a transition. We can't tell my son, "Alright, Garrett. It's bedtime. Now go to bed." He will not operate that way! He needs his transition; he needs to know that he has five minutes to transition between environments. And much like Mr. Rogers—who changed into his cardigan and loafers to transition—we have a bedtime routine. We get my son in the right state of mind for bedtime and rest. I feel like we lose that as we become adults; we feel like we need to jump into things.

Transitions are critical because they get us in the right state of mind to be the best version of ourselves. Play Rebels not only understand that and practice it, but they also use these transitions to be playful. Most people take a break at work, but they use it to check email, catch up on correspondence, or do extra work. Is that really a break?

When play rebels take a break, they have their playlist of things that bring them joy. For example, somewhere near my emergency clown nose, I always have Legos handy. So, if I take a break, I set a timer, take a ten-minute break, and happily build with Legos. Again, it's all about the process, not the outcome, and it powers me up; it gets me in the right state so that I can jump into the next thing fresh and ready to go.

## Schedule Play

Scheduling play is a tough one. When scheduling play is essential, it seems counterintuitive. We tend to live and die by our calendars these days, and what is prioritized gets scheduled. But the reality is, we've conditioned ourselves over the years not to play. So, planning playtime will make it a priority, and keep that promise to ourselves. For me, if it's on my calendar, I'm doing it; if it's not there, good luck! I love to create little pockets of time throughout my day just for doing playful activities.

I learned about a Blank Check for Play from my client Chris Bailey. When it came time for his scheduled play, he would go to the specific items on his Playlist. For example, he would schedule time out of his day specifically to paint or work on a puzzle. But when it came time to have recess with himself, he felt like those things weren't a good fit. So, instead of pressuring himself to do something he wouldn't have fun doing or (sigh) checking email, he created a blank check for play. If he did something playful, no matter what that activity was, he still got the energy he needed to rejuvenate.

# Celebrations: Especially Tiny Wins

If you can roll back time in your memories and think about when we were kids, everything we did was a learning experience. Every day we learned something different, no matter how small, and we got a kick out of just having the experience. And when we learn something, it's important to celebrate. When we celebrate, dopamine rushes through our brains. Dopamine gives us those good feelings of pleasure and satisfaction. And because dopamine is part of the brain's reward system, you subconsciously want to do more of what created that feeling.

As we become adults, we forget about what it's like to learn. We forget what it's like to get better at something. And we save our victories for the epic wins, like when we finally reach retirement or get that house. But by the time we attain the success to celebrate, we're already burned out. To power yourself up, stay on track to reach your goals, and keep in the playful, positive mind frame; anytime you can celebrate—do it!

For example, my son is learning his letters. He spotted an S the other day and pointed out that it was an S. Well, you would've thought that he had found the cure for cancer! My wife and I said, "Oh my gosh, you're so intelligent! That is awesome!" We were celebrating the little guy, and he had the biggest grin of triumph on his face. It feels incredible to celebrate a win. That's something that we can give ourselves that we all too often don't. Now the question is, what small victory can you celebrate today?

# Play Personalities

Once you've come up with your play history, you'll probably notice an affinity toward certain types of activities during play. Those activities give you an idea of what Play Personality you are. Dr. Stuart Brown identified eight Play Personalities in his book. I also utilize the Connector Play Personality that Gwen Gordon references in her writings. Like most people, you're likely to be a mix of different play personalities, but we usually have one or two dominant ones.

Your play personality might change as you age, too, so you should always be open to experimenting with different play activities. Knowing your current or dominant play personality can help you identify the activities that bring true joy into your life and make your play effective and productive. The nine Play Personalities are:

1.    **The Joker**
2.    **The Kinesthete**
3.    **The Explorer**
4.    **The Competitor**
5.    **The Director**
6.    **The Collector**
7.    **The Artist/Creator**
8.    **The Storyteller**
9.    **The Connector**

**The Joker:** Your play always revolves around fun nonsense. You enjoy practical jokes or always have a joke to tell to entertain those around you. You're comfortable being silly and delight in making people laugh.

**The Kinesthete:** You feel playful when you are moving, whether that is through athletics, yoga, dance, or even jumping rope. You may like competition, but as a kinesthete, the goal of these activities is just pure movement.

**The Explorer:** You love to explore new places or gather new experiences through travel, adventure, research, or diving into different points of view. You may also enjoy exploring your inner world through meditation, psychedelic drugs, music, or simple movement.

**The Competitor:** You like specific rules and playing to win. You feel exhilarated when competing on a sports field, a board game, in the boardroom, or even competing against yourself.

**The Director:** You enjoy organizing, planning, and orchestrating events. You love being the one in charge and planning out others' roles. You're comfortable being the center of attention.

**The Collector:** You play by gathering the most interesting objects or experiences. You may travel the world to collect cultural experiences or surround yourself with things like clothing, equipment, memorabilia, or the latest technology gadgets. You also enjoy collecting exciting experiences, like traveling to each continent.

**The Artist/Creator:** You love to make things, whether it's something beautiful, something functional, or even something silly. It may include gardening, cooking, cutting hair, or music. You may never show anyone your creation, but your intrinsic joy is found in the act of creating and self-expression.

**The Storyteller:** Your play focuses on fantasy and imagination. You may love to perform or write or do improv theater. You immerse yourself in literature and movies and enjoy feeling the emotions and experiences of the characters.

**The Connector:** You love most forms of social play, whether it's a good party, networking, a religious or spiritual ritual, a political rally, or a barn raising. You don't need to be in charge, but if it involves connections and the sense of being part of a tribe or community, for you, it's play.

So, look back at the Playlist you made in the last chapter and start to focus on the activities that brought you the most joy. Now you can get a little bit more detailed and ask yourself, "How did that type of play make me feel? Did it make me feel more connected or energized? Was I being creative? Planning something? Moving or competing?"

These reactions to different types of play are how your Play Personalities manifest. Separate your Playlists into things that power you up or power you down. Then dive deeper and sort them according to your Play Personalities. You can make one for the times you need to feel creative by cooking something or drawing. Maybe you need to be focused for a big meeting with a competitor; try using activities from your Playlist that fit a Competitor Personality. Keep a Kinesthete Playlist ready for when you need to be energized and agile. Then, when you have a moment of play, and you need that power-up or to get into a specific mind frame, pull out the list that best fits the need.

## Creating a Recipe for Success

Creating recipes is a way to stack playful routines and recondition ourselves by giving us a guide, or recipe, for directing and controlling our energy levels in a positive way. It increases the likelihood that you'll repeat the behavior because you're more likely to be successful if you follow a recipe. Likewise, if you celebrate a successful repetition of each recipe, you're more apt to repeat the habit. It's a self-repeating upward spiral!

In BJ Fogg's book, Tiny Habits, he says that people who celebrate everything, including small victories, were three times more likely to continue developing a habit, even if they were ordinarily pessimistic people.

Your recipe will have three parts:

1. After I _____,
2. I will _____
3. Because it will make me feel _____.

For example:

1. After I finish a tough meeting,
2. I will immediately take a five-minute walk and focus on my environment.
3. Because it will make me feel calm.

Now, each time you complete your recipe, it gives you a reason to pat yourself on the back, give that self-high-five, or just shout, "Hell yeah!" The positive reinforcement gives us our D.O.S.E. and gets us ready for more of the same.

What we're doing is creating reasons to play. Alongside your Playlist (which I hope you're still adding to when you find new or remember old ways to have fun) try creating a list of things you can do to celebrate in the moment. Maybe it's a little happy dance or saying, "Yippie-ki-yay!" Think about what gives you that D.O.S.E.

Usually, when we think about celebrations, we tend to think about things on a grander scale. For instance, we'll say to ourselves, "I did great this week, so I'm going to treat myself to a spa day!" Don't get me wrong; you should treat yourself to a spa day for doing great. However, if you want to reinforce habits, the celebration needs to happen immediately; it can't be delayed until the end of the week. Stacking small celebrations that culminate in a spa day will be more effective, keep you more invested in improving, and provide better results in the long run.

Ok, Play Rebel, this time I'm giving you a two-part Mission; I know you can handle it! First, I'd like you to take a deep dive into your Playlist and decide which Play Personalities best fit your activities during play. You may fit neatly into one category or be a bit of two or three different types. The goal here is to make you more aware of using different types of Play to gain your desired results and direct your energy.

The second part of the mission is to make a recipe for yourself. Use the three-part formula:

1. After I _____,
2. I will _____
3. Because it will make me feel _____.

Example: *After I finish work on Friday, I will schedule my Play breaks for the next week because it will make me feel pumped on Monday.

Create a recipe that will help you build a habit to direct your energy. Now that you have your recipe, congratulate yourself! Celebrate that victory you just accomplished, Play Rebel. You. Are. AWESOME!

In the next chapter, I'll show you how we can keep joy in our lives even when our situation or circumstances are less than perfect.

RADICAL
ACCEPTANCE
OF REALITY

CHAPTER 5:
# RADICAL
# ACCEPTANCE
# OF
# REALITY

# CHAPTER 5: RADICAL ACCEPTANCE OF REALITY

## Acceptance is Not on Your Terms. It's About Accepting the Offer Before You.

As adults, we have a vision of how we want things to be, and when the situation doesn't align perfectly with that vision, it can be frustrating. But the reality is that there are things within and outside of our control. For instance, we can't control how the weather will be or how people will act. Changing the situation is not always possible, but we can accept what the invitation offers. We can control some of the important stuff, including how we respond to our lack of control. Once we take a situation for what it is, we can control our reactions and move through it.

In the world of improv, we like to say, "Everything is an offer." When we're doing a scene, we may think we're on the same page when that's not the case at all. For example, I may say, "Wow, it's a beautiful night out." My scene partner might respond with, "Yeah, look at the stars. You know, they're so beautiful!" But I may have been hoping that they would say something else, so, at that point, I have two choices. First, I could try to "fix" it by trying to control what my partner said—something like, "No, I wanted you to say something else!" That won't solve the problem, and it would ruin my scene because I couldn't accept the situation.

The other option I have is to say to myself, "All right, this is what they said, gotcha," and go with it. In other words, I accept the offer my scene partner has presented, and we move the scene along. The number one rule of improv is to say "Yes." I like to add an "and" to that, too, so it becomes "Yes, and..." That means that you say yes to the offer, and you build on it.

Going back to our improv scene, if someone says, "Oh, wow, what a beautiful night outside," and you say, "What are you talking about? It's not night. We're in the living room!" Yes, that might get a laugh, but you deny the "reality" of the situation. Instead, in improv, we say something like, "Yes, it is! Oh, yeah, it is a beautiful night, and look at the moon, look at the stars." Again, you accepted the offer, and you built on it by mentioning the stars and moon.

Now, when I started doing workshops, some of my mentees said, "Well, that's nice. But in the real world, you can't always say yes to everything." And they're right. We can't always say yes to everything. But you can accept the situation. That's why I changed the "yes" to "accept and build" or "Yes, and…" You can accept what someone says and let them know they've been heard, then move through the situation.

## Shift Your Mindset

One of my main goals going into 2020 was getting on more stages, doing more demos, and getting in front of more people. I wanted to get people to experience my program because the more they experienced it, the more familiar they got, and the more likely they would reach out to me. I wanted people to experience first-hand how Play could benefit them.

My grand plan abruptly came to a halt with the global pandemic! I went from having my schedule booked with workshops and in-person speaking engagements to having nothing. At first, it was very frustrating, and I felt like I was right back to square one again. But then I had to realize, "All right, I need to surrender and accept the reality before me." The truth was that we weren't doing anything in person, as much as I wanted to change that. Still, once I accepted the situation, I had the opportunity to build on it. I said, "Yes, I can no longer do face-to-face engagements, and now I have the opportunity to work on my web conferences and even write a book!"

Once I accepted the situation and decided to build on it, I got a burst of creativity. I started coming up with new ideas because I allowed myself to go forward with the situation. Don't get me wrong, the purist in me was fighting! It said, "No, this stuff needs to be in-person. How can we create a connection in a virtual environment?" There was a lot of resistance, I'll be honest. When you accept the reality around you, I'm not saying that it's just going to be a walk in the park. However, once you do, it gives you a path to move forward.

In her TED Talk, Jane McGonigal spoke about gamers being more optimistic than most people, even though they fail more times than anyone. But when you're in a play-like state, and things don't go your way, you don't just throw your hands in the air and say, "Well. I guess this was a lost cause; forget it." Instead, you see other ways, try different things; you adjust to the situation.

That's something we can all do when we are conscious of our

Playful Spirit. Think about any game you've played, whether it's a sport, board game, or puzzle. If a challenge or obstacle presented itself or when things didn't go your way, you had to accept the reality. Still, you kept going, trying different solutions, because you were playing. You accepted the outcome and moved on.

# You Are Perfect Just the Way You Are

Coach Dave Buck taught me that our superpowers, our innate strengths, probably got us in trouble sometime in our past. After that, we learned to hide those superpowers because they got us in trouble. Once we reach adulthood, we spend the rest of our lives trying to rediscover what those superpowers were. That's why you're perfect just the way you are. That doesn't mean that we need to stay the same forever. Of course, you're going to learn and grow, but perfection is always there, just like your superpowers.

These days, starting from elementary school, we often feel like we must "fit in" or be just like everybody else. Many educational institutions are looking for the "standard." They want students to fit into a mold. Those left outside that mold often feel like outsiders or even that they're not good enough. But we don't want everyone to be the same in real life because that would be highly ineffective and, quite simply, boring. Looking back on the team activities I've participated in, we weren't great because the team members were all the same. We were great because we brought our true selves to to the table. Our strengths helped complement each other's, and we were successful because we were diverse.

When I first learned that I had ADHD, I thought something was wrong with me for a while, but then I realized that it also gave me some superpowers! Even though it can be challenging to deal with my ADHD sometimes, I can be very charismatic, focus when I want to, and be highly creative. I also have a great sense of humor and a lot of energy. Those two, in particular, got me disciplined in school a lot, so I thought clowning around was something I shouldn't do. But once I became an adult, I learned that I was a crucial energetic presence on many of my teams, precisely because of these superpowers.

## Mistakes Are Gifts

**"I have not failed 10,000 times. I have not failed once. I have succeeded in proving that those 10,000 ways will not work. When I have eliminated the ways that will not work, I will find the way that will work."
—Thomas Edison.**

A failure moment can be something as tiny as a bit of a stumble getting off the elevator, or it can be something like forgetting to pay your phone bill. Most importantly, we want to break out of that negative emotion, that "Oh my gosh—I just messed up!" moment. I like to use something called a failure balance that I learned doing improv. When my group is doing improv, we celebrate failure. And we teach ourselves how to fail—because that's what happens in improv. It's a natural part of the learning process. What we do instead is make that so-called fail a cause for celebration. We might shout, "TA-DAA!" do a little victory dance or take a bow, but we change that adverse, knee-jerk reaction into a win—a gift.

It's natural to celebrate a gift. When you make a mistake and celebrate it, you start to take the negative emotions out of the experience. It becomes easier to disassociate from the negativity of the event because you're not a failure; you're celebrating. You may have failed, but you're not a failure! It's much more effective to look at what new opportunities that error has opened.

Celebrate the opportunity to learn because we can make learning fun through Play. That's where the "gift" part of failing comes in. When we fail, we create opportunities for ourselves to learn. We know that the learning process becomes faster and more understandable when Play gets thrown in the mix, so when we fail, we give ourselves the gift of Play!

## Joy & Grief Can Coexist

I know Play Rebel; not everything is going to be sunshine and rainbows all the time. There are going to be moments when you are not going to be your best. But these complex emotions can coexist as a duality. For instance, after my ex-business partner and I separated, my wife and I realized that we had to move from our house in a minuscule amount of time. That was a hard thing to deal with, and a lot of processing had to happen.

My wife and I decided the best course of action was to sell everything we own and move in with my parents to regroup. But the moment we accepted that this is the reality of a new path, it became easier to find joy in the situation. Two years later, we are renting a different house in another neighborhood. We recently talked about how much better this place is than the one we moved out of so quickly! And we feel like we got lucky when we found this home.

I know these things may sound cliché, and there are some life events in which it's easier said than done to accept reality. But when you have a radical acceptance of reality, you're able to let go of your baggage, all the things that hold you down. And by committing to joy, you allow yourself to keep going. It gives us something on the other side that we can move towards.

By this time, you're starting to recalibrate your Compass of Joy, so when you go through a rough patch, remind yourself of something you used to do that brought you joy. Then find a way to incorporate that activity in some way, shape, or form in your life—especially when you're going through a difficult period.

I rediscovered Legos when my business partner and I had our falling out. I started to fit playtime with them back into my life, and it helped me "put the pieces back together!" The point was not to do anything specific, only to have a moment of enjoyment.

A moment where I didn't need to be completely present, ruminating on what could be or what had happened. I just wanted to recapture that feeling of joy I got—my D.O.S.E.—from simply performing that activity.

## Embracing Failure

In her 2010 TED Talk, Jane McGonigal speaks about urgent optimism. Urgent optimism is the desire to immediately tackle an obstacle, combined with the belief that we have a reasonable hope of success. Gamers subscribe to this concept; they almost always believe an epic win is possible if they just keep trying. And honestly, if there were no obstacles in a video game, it would be boring! It's the same with sports and puzzles—just about everything. If everything were perfect on the first attempt, why would we even bother trying? As adults, we forget about this. We forget about the journey. We want things perfect, and we want them now, just like Veruca Salt in Charlie and the Chocolate Factory.

We won't be perfect at everything we try right away, and that's completely normal. Life will always throw us a curveball. But embracing failure allows a Play Rebel to grow, learn, and have fun along the way. When we practice urgent optimism and seek out the joy in our situation, we can celebrate opportunities to play in life. That lets us create the opportunity to embrace the environment we're in as part of our journey—our learning experience.

# You Can Be a Mess; You Just Can't Stay There

Something that I often remind myself of: there will be days that go better than others, and it's okay to be a mess; you just can't stay there. Too many people these days don't hear that enough. They get to that tough spot and then think, "Oh, I'm a failure because I'm a mess. And now there's no way out of it. And I don't know what to do." It's just a downward spiral. But during an episode of depression, it's easy to forget that we have a choice to remain in that failure mindset or not. When we are in those moments, it's all about choices.

I like to think of it as a choose-your-own-adventure, remember those? From my own experiences of going down both roads, I know that we're not the best version of ourselves when we are in that moment of doom and gloom. We tend to see the world through a very dark lens, and in turn, that viewpoint gets projected onto yet more of the world around us.

But there are other options for seeing the world that are equally valid if you open yourself up to the possibilities. There must be a moment of decision when you choose not to stay there—to move forward again. That's one reason it pays to have playmates and people in your corner that ultimately see the best version of you, even when you don't feel that way. I like to say there's a difference between a friend that is nice and a kind friend. A nice friend will say, "Oh, that's terrible," but then just wallow in the depresssion with you. That's comforting, don't get me wrong. It may give you some sympathy, but it's not going to help you get out of it.

A kind friend will empathize with you and say, "Alright, you know, I hear you, I see you in this terrible spot." They acknowledge you, and then they want to help you build on that acceptance. Remember our "Yes, and..."? A kind friend follows that acknowledgment by building you up again. They may say something like, "Alright, well, what can we do? How do we move forward?"

Now, I'm not saying that you immediately need to do this! Everyone is going to get through the difficult times in life at their own pace. Practice is the key to this step. Practice deciding to move on from the mess. Eventually, those spirals will last from weeks to days, hours, and finally, moments. The process and practice of choosing to move on from the mess of a failure give you a new perspective. That perspective can allow you to turn breakdown moments into breakthrough moments. Accepting and building on your mistakes lets you open up to seeing things differently and retelling your own story.

## Let Go of the Mess and Follow the Message

An important question to ask yourself during a moment of failure is, "What is the message, here?" "How is this helping me become even more powerful?" For example, I have ADHD, but I wasn't diagnosed with it until well into my twenties. It was very frustrating, as a kid, to get in trouble for things I didn't know how to build on. I was the one who took forever to do homework, was always getting in trouble in class or interrupting. I did all that because it was more fun to connect with my classmates than sit down and focus on what I was supposed to do.

I look back at those times, at all that stuff the adults told me was a bad thing, and now I can say to myself, "Oh, this is actually a superpower! Oh, cool!" I realized I could focus if I wanted to, and I've learned that my chattering and interruptions in the classroom translate to charisma and excellent communication skills in the business world! But it wasn't until I got older that I realized that maybe something was medically wrong. So, I went to the doctor and got diagnosed. The diagnosis was validating, but it didn't change anything; I was still me.

It took a while, but I could follow the message once I let go of the mess. The message was that my diagnosis—or even my ADHD itself—didn't make me less; it made me an even better version of myself! Again, Play Rebel, go ahead and get creative in how you build on each obstacle. When you put yourself in a playful mindset, your creativity will kick in, then ask yourself what your personal "Mess" is and look for ways you can choose to accept your mess and use it as a playful opportunity to grow. Sometimes you learn more from your failures than you do from your successes.

## Comparison Is the Thief of Joy

NASA did a study that measured the creativity levels of kids as they progressed from kindergarten through high school. In kindergarten, more than 90% of the kids tested showed genius levels of creativity. But by the time they were seniors in high school, only a staggering 3% retained those high levels of creativity. Those kids had started to compare themselves with other people and suppressed their creativity to conform with those around them. In doing so, they were also stifling their playful spirit and, most importantly, their innate joy.

Around the time you start to become self-aware, usually during puberty, you begin to become more aware of those around you. Most of us also begin to develop a negative internal dialogue too.

That inner voice that tells us it's not true when we think we're creative. That negative voice becomes the whole story if we're not careful. We tell ourselves, "I'm not creative. I can't do it. I'm not good enough." And then we start to believe it, and it becomes our reality. It's sad, but unfortunately true.

I went to school with a guy named Mark. He was a fantastic artist! I mean, he was just so remarkable at a young age, and I didn't know about innate talent or that you could get better at that stuff with practice. I thought that I couldn't draw because I wasn't as good as Mark. I thought, "Obviously, that guy could draw," but my ability was nowhere near his level. So, I just stopped trying. It wasn't until years later that I learned about the NASA study. I suddenly realized I could draw! My drawing may not be the same as Mark's, but I can draw in my style.

It comes down to this, Play Rebel, and I'm honored to repeat it: you're perfect just the way you are! We just need to let ourselves be our natural, playful selves! We often take our inner child and hide it away in a tower and throw away the key. We do this to protect ourselves because we know our playful spirit is vulnerable. But it's that same vulnerability that helps to drive our creativity and guide us through adversity.

# Play Rebel Mission # 4 !

Okay, Play Rebel, it's time for the mission. For this chapter, I'd like you to set aside some time to reflect on something you recently experienced. Something you considered to be a failure. How can you reframe that failure to see the message and use it as a growth opportunity? Write your thoughts down, and the next time you feel like you failed, try this exercise again. Keep practicing; eventually, you won't even have to write it out, and don't forget to keep scheduling your Play Breaks!

MAKING
CONNECTIONS

# CHAPTER 6:
# MAKING
# CONNECTIONS

# Chapter 6: Making Connections

## Recruiting Playmates

It's vital to recruit your friends, colleagues, and family members to be playmates to help you in your epic game of life. I love this quote from the book Superbetter, "It's hard to be vulnerable and ask for help with a serious problem. But it's easy to invite someone else to play a game." Your playmates are people that you can turn to for support and connection. They are people you can speak to honestly about your struggles and challenges and people whom you believe you could ask for help with a troubling problem. You don't need a large squad; having one or two close playmates will be plenty.

Things you can do with your playmates:
- O They can give you a playful challenge to help you level up or overcome a struggle.
- O You can brainstorm strategies with your playmates for conquering a quest.
- O Playmates celebrate wins together.
- O You can have a virtual or in-person play date.
- O Playmates keep you conscious of and accountable for your goals.

Our playmates are our allies in life, and we should try to be allies in return for our playmates. When you reflect on your circle of playmates, it's a good idea to discover how a particular person helps you and how you help them along. This knowledge strengthens our connection to those people and deepens our appreciation for our playmates.

Playmates also aid us in getting our D.O.S.E. We receive oxytocin and dopamine when we socialize. And when we participate in social activities, our mind stays agile and cognitive function improves. Our risk of dementia lowers, and our mental processes are less likely to decline when we participate in group activities, too!

It's easy to feel discouraged when trying to make a connection, so don't be afraid to try more than once. I love the movie The Sandlot. It's a great example of how self-doubt can get in the way of both having playmates and playing. When Scotty Smalls moves to town, he stays inside for the first few weeks, alone in his room.

The reason he's not outside playing, even though it's summer and school is out, is because Smalls has convinced himself that he's just an "egghead" and no good at baseball. But his mother comes to the rescue and encourages him to keep trying by getting outside more.

Smalls' mom has taken on the role of a playmate by helping him through his trouble and urging him to try again. It enables him to befriend Benny "The Jet" Rodriguez, who becomes one of his new playmates.

Transitioning that mentality to the workplace can be more challenging because we don't choose those playmates. Often, we aren't our authentic selves at work, which can present a challenge when connecting with our colleagues. For example, in a brainstorming meeting, the company's job is to be innovative and develop new ideas. If everyone participating is self-conscious about being themselves and is uncomfortable with their environment, that meeting won't be very productive. Ideas won't flow freely, creativity gets stifled, and there may even be some bickering.

But you can create a playground where your colleagues can be comfortable being their "true selves." Your goal is to create an environment where people feel like they belong and can trust each other. When people are on a playground, they become more open to connecting and bonding as playmates. So, playmates at work can make the work itself feel less stressful.

Back when I worked at a digital marketing agency, we had this particularly ruthless client. She was incredibly mean during all our interactions, and we all felt like those meetings were a form of torture! But my colleagues and I were playmates, too, and we had each other's backs. Unbeknownst to our client, we started playing a game we named Buzzwords Bingo. We had a list of marketing terms that this client loved to throw around, and we would keep track of when she said them during each meeting. If we got a blackout on our cards, we would celebrate by having drinks afterward!

Making our environment into a playground and creating our game helped us be more focused. We were paying more attention to what was going on. But more importantly, when that client would lash out at us, as she liked to do, we knew that we had each other's backs. And together, we got through it. So, setting up a playful environment wherever you go is an essential step in helping your colleagues become your playmates.

# Making the Connection

Once you have your playful environment, it can be intimidating to take that first step in connecting with the people around you, especially in the workplace. Typically, when we're at the water-cooler, we have a standard set of social scripts. We usually say, "How are you?" or "How's the weather?" to be polite. We're not seriously expecting a response other than maybe a nod and smile. And when someone else uses these, we may respond, but we're not seriously connecting.

In her book Captivate: The Science of Succeeding with People, Vanessa Van Edwards discusses creating a conversation "spark" instead. She says that whether you're an introvert or extrovert, the critical part of starting that connection is to find an alternative to the typical and mundane social scripts. She suggests using a question that may "spark" the conversation by getting the other person to think about their response. For example, instead of saying, "How are you?" or "Nice day, huh?" you might try "Are you excited for the coming holiday?" or "Is there something this weekend you're looking forward to?"

Rather than simply giving a social script response, such as "Good" or "Yeah, nice day." Now the other person has a reason to start thinking of positive images. By using something outside the norm, you're creating a safe environment for that person to respond. They're also getting a D.O.S.E. because they're thinking of things and activities they're excited about and anticipating. Now you can connect with your new playmate on a deeper level because you've opened a playful space for them in which to feel safe.

You can also choose activities outside of the norm to break the ice. Instead of the standard coffee or lunch meeting, try inviting a new acquaintance to play catch or go for a walk around the block. I've found that activities like these help us to connect on a deeper level. (I save money when I do this, so this technique helps my wallet, too!)

From there, it's: wash, rinse, and repeat until you and your Play Rebel Crew rule the office! Seriously, though, playmates are essential when you're in a setting like a business meeting where you need to be productive as a team. A group of people who aren't playmates will feel more stressed, not get along as well, and won't get as much done.

Understanding what energy you're bringing to the situation is essential, too. You may be scared, nervous, or just impatient. But there's a difference between reaction and response. Your initial reaction may be fear, withdrawal, or hesitation. However, you can choose how you respond. If you go into a situation with the spirit of joy and a positive outlook, it will affect the outcome! If you simply think about how that connection will benefit you and others, and acknowledge your initial emotions, you can control your response to the environment.

Case in point, I remember doing a workshop for a professional sports team for their sales organization. That field can be highly competitive, and they wanted their team to feel more like a team. We started playing some games during the workshop, and at the beginning of the session, I could tell people were just not into the playful spirit! Some of them were standing with arms crossed, obviously not interested. Now, these games are ridiculous, but they all have a more profound function.

During one activity, I had people walk around the space and imagine different scenarios. One of them was to imagine that everyone that they met was "icky". I told them to ignore anyone in their vicinity actively. Then I had them do the opposite of that. They were to imagine that anyone they met was a best friend that they hadn't seen in a long time.

During the discussion later, I asked the group specifically about the exercise to ignore everyone. I asked them to raise their hand if it felt normal when they were doing this exercise. Several people raised their hands, and then I asked the question, "How many people didn't feel comfortable doing that one?" Again, several of them raised their hands. Then this one woman spoke up and said, "Yeah, when we did that one, I felt alone, like I didn't belong here—anonymous." I asked her to elaborate, and she said this exercise made her feel like people didn't want her there.

That triggered a VP in attendance to raise their hand. They had realized that they normally went about their day like that! At that moment, this VP concluded that they were causing a wave of despair by making people feel alienated. This VP was only doing their job, but they were trying to look busy and important. They would rush through the office looking incredibly determined and businesslike, usually on their phone, not acknowledging their colleagues or even making eye contact. What they hadn't realized was that they were making their colleagues feel "icky" like in the exercise.

Something as simple as making eye contact or smiling allows people to connect. The energy they brought to the environment made a huge difference. Oh, and that sales team? By the end of the day, you would think a completely different team was attending my workshop! They became more open to being playmates and started to connect. By the end of the day, this sullen dysfunctional team was high-fiving and cheering each other on to even more outstanding achievements!

## We > Me

When I'm doing improv, it's all about the ensemble. If you're focusing on yourself, you're not going to help push the story along. Remember, "Everything's an offer." You need to accept the offer if you're going to participate in the interaction. That's true everywhere else, too, even in the workplace.

Let's go back to The Sandlot. When Smalls hit the ball that he took from his stepdad over the fence, the rest of the group came together to celebrate his win. Then they want to understand why Smalls wasn't celebrating his home run. When they find out how important that baseball is, they pull together to try and figure out how to get it back. After a series of misadventures, including erector sets, giant slingshots, and hoists, they finally succeed by working together.

The point that I'm making here is that when you put your heads together and create a safe space to be playful in, you're going to come up with better ideas than anyone could have come up with on their own. The next time you're throwing ideas around with your team, try to figure out how to incorporate your thoughts with someone you may not usually agree with. This trains you to accept someone's idea and build on it. You don't necessarily have to love your coworker's idea; you just need to acknowledge the offer. Remember, in improv, everything's an offer. Once that offer presents itself, you need to build on it. I'm confident you'll be able to create some fantastic ideas that you wouldn't have come up with on your own.

In other words, we are the average of the people in our network. I'm incredibly fortunate that I have amazing people in my network. They've lifted me to support me when I'm down; they inspire me. My playmates help me brainstorm and want to see me achieve my dreams. To put it another way, I rely on my playmates' superpowers. I ask, "What are they super good at and enjoy doing that helps me in some way?" I also try to think about how to engage with that person so I can be a better playmate. I try to think of ways to move the task at hand to the Playground.

Once my team is there, we can be playmates and allies. If you are a manager, a way to connect and learn their superpowers is to play a game with your team. By watching them play, you'll start to know about your team's temperaments and personalities.

I used to have my groups play a board game, like Monopoly, to understand how each team member handles challenging situations. How do they strategize? How do they organize? When we finished the game, I could describe my team's superpowers more accurately and support them where they needed.

You can't play a team sport, like football or baseball, by yourself. You need other people to help you. That's natural during play. I remember growing up playing Super Mario Bros, and my friends and I would strategize every week—"What did you do?" "How did you level up?" "How did you beat Bowser?" We were asking for help but in the spirit of the game. Everyone felt like they were contributing, and all our ideas came together to be better than just one person's brainstorm because we were connecting on a deeper level.

# You Are the Average of the People in Your Network

Through my coaching, I learned about the Seven Influential People exercise. We can all relate to feeling like things are just effortless when you're in a group of friends. But in other circles, it's all doom and gloom. I learned from a mentor that you're the average of the people you surround yourself with. That includes people you know personally, people in your virtual network, and even things you read.

Doing the Seven Influential People audit will help you reach your outcome when you engage in activities with a group. First, you'll need to decide what your desired outcome is. You know, what are you trying to accomplish with this activity? Then, while you're auditing your network, try finding ways for your playmates to contribute to your success.

That's why I like to find out what my playmates' superpowers are. I ask: "How can that playmate be my ally as I'm going through this big game of life?" I remind myself that people genuinely want to help people.

At the end of the day, most people want you to succeed. But we're often scared to ask for help because we think we're going to be a nuisance or bothersome. So, by asking for help, or getting someone to use their superpowers to help you, it's a win/win situation. Your playmate will be doing something they're naturally skilled at, which makes them feel good. They get a D.O.S.E. just by helping you, and you're getting assistance.

When you play, your standard rules go out the window so you can have fun on your Playground. When we're engaged in play, our brain will actively avoid logic and critical thinking, such as watching a science fiction movie or playing a game with a dragon as a character. We know dragons aren't real, but we set that logic aside so we can enjoy ourselves. I mean, let's face it, it's more fun

to slay the dragon than not play because dragons aren't real! This behavior is called suspension of disbelief, or sometimes willing suspension of disbelief.

We can use suspension of disbelief to our advantage when we create our Playground in the workplace. We can't choose who our workmates are, and we may not necessarily even like them, but we must work together and be productive as a team. The cool thing about using play in the workplace is that it allows people to suspend the disbelief that they aren't in a work environment. They can connect, get closer, trust each other more, and get the work done while still finding joy in it because they're willing to set aside the logic that "work isn't fun."

Even though you're just playing a game, your brain doesn't need to know the difference between the Playground and reality. Because you and your teammates are helping each other, your brain tells you that those other people are playmates. Your subconscious tells you, "I must like that person; I must respect that person. I'm helping them and furthering the game, so they must be my playmate."

In Superbetter, Jane McGonigal talked about a couple whose families hated each other. The in-laws fought with each other all the time, making the couple's life miserable. One thing they all had in common, though, was that they were all playing Farmville on Facebook. In this game, you and your connections on Facebook get opportunities to help each other and tend to each other's farms. Doing this gains you more points, too. So, in the spirit of the game, the in-laws of this family would do things to help the others play. They suspended the belief that they were feuding to further the game and acted like playmates—allies.

This behavior started to ripple into their activities outside the game, too. They became more understanding of each other. They were more supportive and listened better, and finally learned to get along. The power of play brought this family together and allowed them to connect and strengthen their bonds as a family!

## Seven Most Influential People Exercise

I adapted this exercise from my coach training at Coachville. The Seven Most Influential People Exercise is the "audit" I mentioned earlier in this chapter.

Think of 3-4 people that you spend the most time with, your family and friends. Those people are your Inner Network.

Now, think of 2-3 people you know who are strategically connected to you in some way, like colleagues or associates.

Make a chart naming the 3-7 people down the left side of

your chart.

Then, make five columns to jot down notes for each question.
Your columns should be labeled:

- Talk
- Energy
- Assets
- Request
- Support

Fill in the columns for each person using the below questions:

**Talk -** What do you talk about most of the time?

**Energy -** What is the overall energy/mood of this person
and relationship?

**Assets -** What assets do they have that you could leverage
better for your success?

**Request -** What could you ask them for that you have
not asked?

**Support -** Rate the level of support they provide
(1 distraction/detractor - 10 maximum supporter)

# Follow-up Questions:

Is there anything you can see to do to get more support from your inner and outer network from doing this exercise?

How can you expand your connection with someone and positively increase their influence on your ability to be more playful?

Here's an example:

| NAME | TALK | ENERGY |
|---|---|---|
| Jake | Psychology, friends, life relationships. | Person: Varies Relationship: Insightful |

| ASSETS | REQUEST | SUPPORT |
|---|---|---|
| Honesty, great at feedback, understands how people work. | Help on relationship and therapy advice | 7 |

Now you can take an "audit" of your network and see where you might add playmates who can support your needs. Don't worry if some of your friends don't support you like you want, though. Unless a person is hurtful somehow, you don't have to cut people out of your life.

When I first started to learn how to eat healthier, I was afraid I would have to give up all my sugary, fatty, unhealthy snacks at once. But that wasn't the case. I started gradually adding in healthy alternatives. Before I knew it, they had replaced most of my unhealthy snacking habits.

So, if you notice a lack of playmates who support you in the way you need, try to connect with some new people who can. See you next chapter, Play Rebel, where we'll be learning how to recognize and accept invitations to play.

# CHAPTER 7:
# SEEK OUT INVITATIONS TO PLAY

# CHAPTER 7: SEEK OUT INVITATIONS TO PLAY

## The Universe Sends Invitations All of the Time

My mentor, Gwen Gordon, talks about how we live in an Enchanted Playground. This Playground is always inviting us to play, but sometimes those invitations are not apparent to us. However, if you have the right mindset, anything can be a form of play. Gwen calls this "Playing with the mystery." Even in situations when you meet with adversity, you're being called to be playful.

For instance, I've been calling the pandemic of 2020 The Great Pause. Before the lockdown, I believed that the work I did had to be in person. That's just how I've always done things. So, when we got shuttered at home, all my appointments and workshops got canceled. I had a moment of despair and panic when I didn't know what I would do.

However, once I took a moment and a breath, I remembered that everything is an invitation to play. I started asking myself the questions, "What could this be calling me to do?" "What would a virtual playground look like?" and that's when I began experimenting with what I could do in this new environment. Once again, I worked on accepting my new reality, then started building by saying to myself, "Yes, and…?"

Here's how I did it. First, I reached out to my network and said, "Hey, I have more time on my end! Who would like to experiment in this virtual space and see how we can create something?" The second thing I did was to get an upgraded Zoom account! After that, I started experimenting. It wasn't perfect, but I saw the possibility! My point here is that, yes, Play Rebels get frustrated; we go through all the complex emotions of setbacks, but we look at a setback as an invitation. The obstacles in our path are invitations to bring our playful mindset to the table and experiment with possibilities.

For example, if we play a video game and something gets in our way, we see it as a fun challenge and keep playing. However, sometimes in life, when a formidable challenge comes our way, we get frustrated or throw our hands in the air and give up. But if we can keep up that "Improv Spirit" by accepting that invitation and saying, "Yes, and…" we give ourselves a better chance of success. We need to "keep playing," so to speak, just like we would in that video game.

Sparking your curiosity is an excellent way to keep that Playful Spirit from faltering! When we get stuck in a rut or bored, we normally don't feel like we're moving as fast as possible. That feeling often spirals into frustration and antipathy, which lead to more stress and burnout. In these situations, I like to invite people to look at the world through another lens. I ask them to imagine they're still a child, seeing the world around them for the first time.

I tell them it takes a little practice at first, but start small, and it gets easier. For instance, don't just zone out on your commute to work. Drive down the road and try to catch something that you never noticed before. Instead of just walking your dog along the same route, go down a path you can both explore a little. This exercise brings out our natural curiosity and sense of wonder. It allows you to get into a playful mindset with less effort.

# Curiosity is Your Ally

Curiosity isn't just my ally; I consider Curiosity one of my superpowers! Curiosity was one of those superpowers nearly drummed out of me as a child because I found myself getting into a lot of mischief (mostly) unintentionally! I was a curious kid; I couldn't help myself. I was always wondering, "What will happen if I do this? What will happen if I go there?"

A funny example is, when I was about six or seven, my family and I lived in an apartment, and one evening, they were watching TV while I was exploring our home. I had wandered into their closet when I suddenly thought, "What does this wall connect to? Can I see through to the kitchen?" So, I got a long screwdriver out of my dad's toolbox and started hammering it through the wall! After a few strikes, I ran into the kitchen to find out if it was poking out yet. It wasn't, so I continued this process—hammering, then running into the kitchen to check for the screwdriver—several times.

Eventually, my mom noticed me running back and forth and pointed it out to my dad. Of course, I got in trouble, and it was a costly mistake for my parents, but the curiosity itself wasn't wrong, only what I did with it. That's the thing. That's the whole point of the exercise—kids are naturally curious. So, if we can recapture that playful curiosity as adults, we can control how we use it. Unfortunately, as we get older, we forget about curiosity and let things like anxiety control us.

# Get Outside of Your Comfort Zone

Sometimes we become discontent with life or start to wonder why we've been so bored for a while. It's often a sign that we haven't been playing enough or that we've come up against a barrier to being playful. We sacrifice our playful spirit to stay in our comfort zone, primarily out of fear. The act of playing is inherently messy and scary. There isn't always a guaranteed outcome, and it won't always work out the way we plan. But if we try to control every aspect of our life or are too afraid of making a mistake, we won't be able to gain the benefits of play at all.

Sure, when I tried my screwdriver experiment, I knew I could get in trouble. But I remember the wonder, excitement, and curiosity when I was playing a whole lot more than I remember what my parents did to punish me afterward. You see, the exciting thing is we are wired to play!

Animals in the wild—mammals, birds, even fish and insects—have been observed playing, too. Even though play can be inherently dangerous in the wild, animals engage in play and are completely present during the activity. The reason for this is that playing keeps us mentally agile. When we get outside of our comfort zone and accept the invitation to play, our creativity goes into overdrive so we can build on our situation.

I discovered a website and book a while ago called Hello Fears. On the site, Michelle Poehler, a woman I greatly admire, talks about her comfort zone. When she was a small child, her eyesight was terrible, so she clung to her mom and stayed close to her whenever possible. This tiny little "safety bubble" was very comfortable for her, so that's where Michelle stayed. Growing up and continuing through high school, she stayed home, rarely tried new things, and didn't like to take risks.

However, when she was in college, she conducted an experiment called: "100 Days Without Fear." During this experiment, Michelle documented 100 days of doing things that scared her. Little by little, she delved outside her comfort zone. Michelle did everything from playing with spiders and skydiving to karaoke with a live band and exploring what it felt like to be old through makeup and prosthetics. She even posed for a nude painting!

When she concluded the experiment, she discovered two things. First, she survived all of it, even though her fears told her she wouldn't. Second, once she achieved her incredible feats of courage, she was able to continue and do even more than she ever thought possible. She was able to accomplish so much by staying in a playful, curious mindset. That playful spirit bolstered her inner strength, and now Michelle helps people worldwide by teaching them how to get out of their comfort zones!
'

The critical thing to understand, Play Rebel, is that getting outside our comfort zone, and even the act of play itself, is inherently disorganized and uncomfortable. There will always be some fear in your life, even if you routinely get outside your comfort zone. But use your curiosity to find the wonder and joy in your situation. You can gain strength through your adversities. I like to say we're not fearless, we just fear less!

I got that quote from another mentor of mine, Judi Holler. She wrote the book Fear Is My Homeboy: How to Slay Doubt, Boss Up, and Succeed on Your Own Terms, and she's also a lover and performer of improv theater. We used to talk about how, as a performer, that fear of getting on stage never entirely leaves for some people. It's always there. Even though we both delight in getting onstage and enchanting an audience without a script, we still get those butterflies before every show. So, I acknowledge that fear. I accept the invitation to play and build on my situation by finding the joy and wonder all around me.

## Play With Disruption in Your Life: Get comfortable with disruption, and accept it as an invitation to be playful!

In his book, Curious? Discover the Missing Ingredient to a Fulfilling Life, Todd Kashdan talks about curiosity being an underutilized emotion. I think that's because it's mainly a reactionary feeling. We're not intentionally curious when we're in a new environment or doing something for the first time; we're not really controlling our reaction. Instead, we tend to run on autopilot, and all too often, this leads to stress—sort of a "fight, flight, or freeze" mentality. Many adults have a hard time enjoying new or strange situations because of this. Their curiosity and creativity get overpowered by their anxiety.

Being in that fear state all the time isn't helpful for anyone, though. When our anxieties take over, the logical side of the brain shuts down. We stop asking questions because panic, although irrational, is deeply rooted in emotion. The advantage of curiosity is that it cuts through that emotion because you need to focus on directing it. Your brain gets forced to ask questions, allowing it to function in a more controlled and logical way.

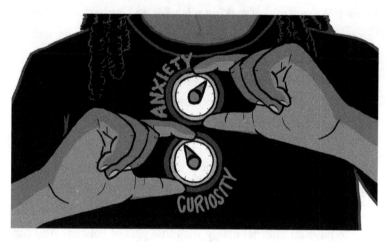

Mr. Kashdan goes on to explain that people have two choices—"knobs," as he calls them. The two knobs are Curiosity and Anxiety. He says that we can use these knobs to adjust our reactions and control our responses to new or uncomfortable situations. Typically, our "Anxiety Knob" gets turned up to a ten in a new environment.

The best way to control that reaction is to turn up your "Curiosity Knob." When you begin to be curious about your situation, your stress levels decrease. You can start to concentrate on accepting the invitation to play. When you get playful under new conditions or in the face of adversity, you can utilize your innate creativity more efficiently and skillfully.

A lot of times, we're scared to be creative because of the unknown. We're afraid of making mistakes and embarrassing ourselves, so fear takes over. When we let our fear control us, we're not reaching our full potential. So, we sometimes need to have a conversation with our fear. But we can't just treat it like a child and tell it to go to bed. And berating yourself won't get a positive response, either. You need to treat that fear with love!

Anxiety and fear are there to help you. Think of those two emotions as loving parents, sometimes a little bit overprotective, but well-meaning. When you visualize your feelings like that, you can start to have an internal dialog with that part of yourself. You can tell that fear or anxiety, "Hey, look, I know that there is a potential for danger. But me and Curiosity, we're going to go out, and we're going to have fun. "We're going to be careful, but Fear, you're not running the show."

I learned this method from Elizabeth Gilbert, who talks more about dealing with fear in Big Magic: Creative Living Beyond Fear. She talks about fear and anxiety in the context of creativity and suggests saying to that part of yourself, "Hey, you know, I appreciate you, thank you for having my back. Right now, though, this isn't helpful. So, you're going in the backseat. You're allowed to come along, but me and Curiosity, we got this."

# Make Meetings/Work Playful

Remember when I talked about the Mary Poppins Effect? For every job that must be done, you find the element of fun, and snap the job's a game! This effect applies to work, too. Naturally, when I talk about this, I always get at least one person that says, "Well, paying your taxes isn't fun! What about all these boring things we have to do as adults?" I totally get it; seriously, I'm not too fond of those things, either.

But try to think about your strengths or the things you enjoy and how you can incorporate those while doing the activity. You can also modify the action so that you can get a bit more joy out of it. I like to say, "When you turn the play switch on, everything gets better." It's kind of the same thing Ms. Poppins was talking about.

For instance, I'm trapped in my office for fifteen months, so I actively seek out invitations to play to create an environment that will breed playfulness. I turn the play switch on and do something out of the ordinary or just plain silly.

Instead of having a regular boring meeting, what if you went through a connection activity to kick off the teamwork? Instead of struggling to do the dishes, try setting a timer, putting on your favorite playlist, and getting lost in the music. That's what my wife does. She has an Apple watch, and she turns it on and works out anytime she's out doing chores. She has music going, and the time just flies. These are just some small ways you can insert some joy and playfulness into your daily activities. Go back to your Play history and take another look at the things that brought you the most joy. Try to find new ways to insert small pieces of those things into your everyday routine.

I used to go to this old theater by my house all the time, and there was this older gentleman named R. B. (One of his pet peeves was when people asked him what the R. B. stood for, so I just didn't.) But this old gentleman was so playful! All he did was take tickets; that was his job, but he was always upbeat. He would talk to you, joke and chat. He saw his work as play.

R. B. had coworkers, so he wouldn't always be there when I showed up, but every time I went to the movie theater, I would hope that he would be working. It just made that experience more fun because I enjoyed his company more than the other ticket takers. Anyhow, I asked R. B. once, "What's your thing? Why are you always so upbeat?"

He replied, "I just love people, you know, and I love coming to work because I get to be around people!" You see, R. B. knew what brought him joy—people—and how to bring that into his work through play. He sought out invitations to play; he looked for that in everything he did. Some of the people doing the exact same job dreaded every shift, and you could tell. They were the ones going through the motions, bored, and no fun to interact with! Emotions are contagious, so when you bring a playful attitude to the table, it helps others join in and livens up any situation, even work. A Playful mindset is simply attractive.

Play Rebel Mission # 6!

Your challenge this week, Play Rebel, is to flip your Play Switch on!

Try to seek out invitations to play in everything you do. Whether you're at home, work, or even if things aren't necessarily going well, try to spy out any invitations that you usually would miss. Write down some ideas for the next time you have an opportunity to slip some playfulness into your life.

Once you find a new invitation, accept it, and build on your situation. And don't forget to search out new Playmates and invite them to play, too! Encourage yourself to be open to the people and possibilities around you, even if you're having a bad day; you never know what might turn into Play!

CHAPTER 8:
# BARRIERS TO PLAY

# Chapter 8: Barriers to Play

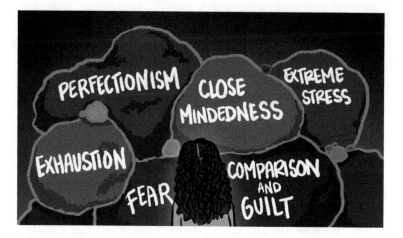

## Play is...

- O Produced in an alert, non-stressed frame of mind. Animals don't play when they are stressed. Stress is an obstacle, a Barrier to play.
- O Intrinsically motivated. We should be playing for pleasure, not gain.
- O Done freely, not coerced. It isn't play if we're forced into it, and addictions shouldn't compel play.

○ Structured by rules we invent. An agreement of having fun is what binds our actions during play, and the rules show us how to do that instead of limiting our behavior.

Most of all, play is fun!

Play is also best achieved when we can be childlike in our behavior rather than childish.

## Childlike vs. Childish

### Childlike

○ Curiosity
○ Wonder
○ Empathy

### Childish

○ Throwing Tantrums
○ Indifference
○ Selfishness

When we act childish, we're actively constructing barriers to our play! Barriers to play often sneak up on us when we're not paying attention. They can start as a little excuse, for example, to not go on your daily walk, and build into a longing to get outside more often faster than we can imagine.

Play is an emotional state, and Barriers take us away from that emotional state; either through physical means, like stress and exhaustion, or through mental avenues, such as perfection and comparison. Some of the most significant barriers to play are also the most common. We've gone over ways to defeat all of them in previous chapters, but now I'll name and review the Barriers to Play because it's essential to stay aware of how they can affect us all.

# The Play Barriers

## Perfection

Dr. Stuart Brown has a lot to say about perfection. He says that play is a state of mind rather than just an activity, and because of that, some people will say that they're playing, but they're actually not. When you compare yourself to someone else or try to be perfect, you're not in that play-like state. You may be going through the motions, but you will end up being frustrated because you deny yourself the chance to be creative and have fun.

Close-mindedness is another manifestation of the perfection barrier. If you believe that there's only one way of doing something, you'll quickly fall into the trap of trying to be perfect and not measuring up to your "ideal." Thinking there's only one way to do things will set you up for inevitable failure when things don't go according to plan. But, when we let go of our expectations, get creative, and start problem-solving through play, we can accept our situation and build on it. We can be more open to things going a different way than we plan.

## Extreme Stress

Stress itself is not a bad thing, but stress is only meant to last for short bursts. Prolonged stress is a negative influence. When stress conditions are maintained for long periods, it leads to a decrease in motivation. Playing and being in a playful state of mind take a back burner because you're not going to want to do anything that brings you joy. Your body is stuck in fight, flight, or freeze mode. You start to get frustrated when you're stressed out a lot, and you're just unsatisfied.

## Exhaustion

Exhaustion is very similar to stress when we're talking about play barriers. When I'm overly stressed, I find that I stop thinking about the future or past and live in the now. This wears me down until I feel so tired, I don't want to do anything, especially play. I get this tunnel vision and begin to find play more of a nuisance. I start to think I don't have time for it because I'm tired or too busy to keep up. The exhaustion and stress barriers will often feed each other or stack up on each other.

## Comparison

Dr. Brown also talks about comparison a lot. According to him, sometimes running is play, and sometimes it's not. The difference between the two depends on the emotions experienced by the runner. Play is a state of mind rather than an activity. Remember, the definition of play is: an absorbing, apparently purposeless activity that provides enjoyment and suspension of self-consciousness and sense of time. Play is also self-motivating, it makes you want to do it again.

We must put ourselves in the proper emotional state to play. So, although an activity can get you into a playful state, if you judge yourself, you're trying too hard not to make mistakes, and you're not playing. Remember, play is inherently messy and an intrinsically vulnerable activity.

## Guilt

Guilt motivates people to repair the damage they've done. In a study about prison inmates, researchers found that criminals who were prone to experiencing guilt suffered more from what they had done than those who didn't feel guilty. As a result, they were more likely to attempt to make amends and fix the problems they caused where possible. — Todd B. Kashdan

Mistakes are necessary for growth, so we've all done things we regret. Guilt can help you acknowledge your responsibilities and motivate you to improve. It can also help teach us what to do differently. In most cases, a little bit of guilt can help to promote positive growth.

But, when we hold onto unhealthy guilt, it can cause both physical and emotional turmoil. Guilt is a powerful emotion. It can manifest as a nauseating twist in your stomach when you've hurt someone else, or recurring self-judgment and criticism related to your past. While ignoring your guilt or trying to push it away might seem like a helpful strategy, unaddressed guilt can build and intensify, making you feel worse over time.

To successfully navigate guilt, you need to recognize where it comes from. It's normal to feel guilty when you know you've done something wrong, but guilt can also take root because of events you didn't have anything to do with. While owning up to mistakes is important, even if you only admit them to yourself, it's equally important to take note when you blame yourself for things you can't control.

You might feel guilty about breaking up with someone who still cares about you, or because you have a good job and your best friend can't seem to find work. Or maybe you just believe you've failed to fulfill someone's expectations. But, when we feel guilty about these sorts of things, we're forgetting about the effort we've put in to overcome our own challenges or keep ourselves healthy! You can't mend every situation, and some decisions or mistakes might cost you a treasured relationship or close friend. But, before you can leave the past behind, you need to accept it. Looking back and ruminating on your memories won't fix what happened.

You can't rewrite events by agonizing over outcomes, but you can consider what you've learned and use it to move through your guilty feelings. Ask yourself:

- What led to the mistake? Explore triggers that prompted your action and any feelings that tipped you over the edge.
- What would you do differently now?
- What did your actions tell you about yourself? Do they point to any specific behaviors you can work on?

Remember guilt can work for you, it can serve as an alarm that lets you know when you've made a choice that conflicts with your personal values. Instead of letting guilt overwhelm you, try putting it to work. Use it as a tool to cast light on areas of yourself you feel dissatisfied with.

# Fear

The fear barrier comes in many different varieties, like the fear that you might fail, for instance, that comes with stepping out of your comfort zone or the fear of being made fun of. There's physical fear like in our running example; you can trip and fall and bust your knee open, right? There are emotional fears, too. Somebody can point at you and say, "Oh, you run funny." Any of those different fears will keep us from getting to our playground because the act of playing is very vulnerable. It's inherently messy. You will make mistakes. That's why people get stuck behind the fear barrier.

Entrepreneur and lifestyle guru Tim Ferriss talks a lot about fear. He poses the question to his audience, "What's the worst possible outcome, and how do I handle that?" When we start thinking about the worst possible outcome and how we might handle it, we use our creativity. That will give us the strength and playful attitude to overcome the fear barrier. Going back to our runner, what's the worst possible outcome? There might be something to trip over, so maybe our runner should wear knee pads.

In fact, do whatever makes you feel more comfortable and helps to prepare for that worst-case scenario. At work, I might stumble on my words or freeze up. That's alright, it's happened; I've frozen in meetings before, so I started taking up improv. If your fear is based on something that happened in the past, you can brainstorm things to put into place that help get around the fear barrier. Don't forget to ask your playmates to help you prep. They can aid you in finding ways to alleviate your fears because they can identify your superpowers.

It's also important to be realistic about the likelihood of your fears coming true. You should assess your anxiety and worry, make sure it's based on the probability of that thing or event actually happening. If not, try to worry less about that specific fear. You know, we might worry about getting bitten by a shark, it's probably best not to worry much about it until we're in the ocean!

# How the Barriers Reveal Themselves

When we feel burnt out, we aren't physically capable of enjoying the act of play. Playing is not something our brain allows when we go into a fight, flight, or freeze survival mode, like when we feel attacked or extremely stressed. The blood is being rushed to our extremities so that we can survive, and the brain goes on autopilot, so playing isn't even a viable option. So, if you're not powering yourself up or getting the rest you need, you won't feel capable or motivated to engage in play.

Just like my dog, Daphne, when she broke her paw and got put in her cast, she went into a fearful, survival mode. She couldn't do the things that she usually could, so as a result, she became easily irritable. She wasn't wholly aggressive; Daphne was only thinking about staying alive. She started nipping at the other dog, and when those play opportunities showed up, she didn't engage in them. Her pain was allowing the fear and stress barriers to stop her from being playful.

## Overcoming Barriers and Play Inhibitors

Barriers more physical in nature, such as extreme stress and exhaustion, often arise when we aren't giving ourselves the care we need. When we haven't powered up, our brain goes into preservation mode, where it takes all the creative areas of our brain offline. This activates the limbic system, also called the lizard brain, whose only job is to keep us alive, not to problem-solve or have fun.

When the lizard brain is active, it could be a sign that maybe there's a challenge to be overcome. Suppose the prospect of playing, or bringing on a playful mindset, immediately repulses, annoys, or makes you feel stressed. In that case, you need to assess your emotions.

The easiest way to do this assessment is to use the first four levels of Maslow's hierarchy of needs. This theory in psychology is used to understand how humans participate in behavioral motivation and is typically portrayed in the shape of a pyramid. In simpler terms: human behaviors, and the reasons behind them, usually

terms: human behaviors, and the reasons behind them, usually move through stages in order, in this case, from the base of a pyramid up to the top.

Each of those stages must be met before you move to the next. There are eight stages, divided into lower or deficiency needs and higher or growth needs. The deficiency or d-needs are lowest on the pyramid and most fundamental; they are called deficiency needs because life becomes unpleasant when we don't have enough of them. The deficiency needs are:

- Physiological Needs
- Safety
- Social Belonging
- Esteem

Next are the growth needs, which are the higher-level needs, both on the pyramid and pertaining to conscious development. These aren't things we need because they're necessary to live; we need them to grow. Because of that, they're called the growth needs:

- Cognitive needs
- Aesthetic needs
- Self-actualization
- Transcendence

Most of the time, Play Rebels don't need to worry about the top four because the very act of play helps achieve them. What we're concerned with for our purposes are the bottom-tier needs. Without satisfying all those needs, a true playful mindset can't be attained.

To do an assessment, you need to ask yourself a series of four questions.

## 1. Are all my physiological needs met?

This includes rest, hydration, health, air, and warmth —all the physical things you need to live.

## 2. Do I feel safe?

To play, you need to feel safe and secure, both

physically and emotionally. This includes security in other areas, such as financial security, health, and wellness, and not being afraid of having a debilitating accident. You don't have to be rich or in perfect health—don't get me wrong—but you don't need to feel like you live in a war zone or that you'll lose your job if you play. If you don't feel safe on at least a basic level, you won't be willing to take the risks necessary to immerse yourself in play completely. You'll go straight into survival mode, and your brain will go back on autopilot.

## 3. Do I feel some sense of social belonging?

Everyone needs social interaction and to feel a sense of belonging on some level in their lives. Emotional intimacy with others, friendship, and family connections can even help us overcome needs lower on the pyramid at times. Such examples are when siblings overcome famine which is a Physiological need or disaster, a Safety necessity, because of their strong bond.

## 4. Do I feel respected and/or adequate?

The need for esteem comes in two forms, the affection or respect of your peers and friends and your self-esteem. While having the respect of your peers is something everyone craves, having high self-esteem can make up for the lack of your social circle.

Answering those questions will give you a solid idea of whether there is a deficit in one or more of those areas—if there's an "imbalance in the Force," as Obi-Wan would say. If you find one, address and tend to it. For example, I started finding myself irritable and short-tempered a while ago. I told myself that I wasn't my usual, playful self. And I know sometimes these things happen, but if they go unchecked, they can turn into serious issues.

So, I started to assess the situation. I asked myself, "Where, in the last couple of days, had my needs not been met?" I'd had several mission-critical things that I had to take care of that ate up a lot of time, and I hadn't been sleeping as much or as long as I needed to. I was waking up early and going to bed later than usual. I said, "Alright, you know what, I'm exhausted!" My physiological needs weren't being met, leading to an exhaustion barrier. All I needed to do was give myself some leeway not to have to work so much. I took a timeout and followed my Compass of Joy. Doing just one fun activity allowed me to get back into that playful spirit.

It's also helpful to look at the activity that makes you unhappy. Sometimes, when you engage in an activity and can't get into a playful mindset, something about that action might build a barrier for you. Perhaps you don't feel good enough or are self-conscious about your ability. In that case, you need to identify those feelings and address them.

Be honest with yourself, and don't be afraid to take a step back and ask for help. You can call on some of your playmates to assist you with these things. If you're scared about the potential outcome, try Tim Ferriss' worst-case scenario exercise. You can even ask your friends to help you plan and give you some great ideas to make you feel more secure.

Sometimes these play barriers start to stack up. For instance, if you're not getting enough sleep, you're probably more likely to be stressed. Adding to that, you'll be less likely to want to play. When you're not playing, you're not creative, which means that you will be very close-minded and less likely to see the things that will help you overcome all those barriers.

## Other Play Inhibitors

While you may want to be playful, your environment may not be conducive to play. In other words, the environment always wins. I learned that phrase from coach school , where I got certified as a professional coach. While I was there, we learned about managing the environment. Take your workplace. Maybe it's very sterile, or the people you work with are grumpy; perhaps it's even a layoff day. Any of those can influence your ability to bring a playful spirit to the table. If you immerse yourself in a hostile environment, your ability to summon a playful mood and find joy in your situation may suffer.

Taking an emotional assessment in different places and times can help you pinpoint if you're up against a classic emotional barrier, like perfectionism, or if something in your environment is triggering the obstacle. If you find that something in your environment is blocking your playground, try to think of ways to make your domain more "play-friendly." Ask yourself what you can do to add some fun to the place you're in.

If the problem is personnel, "How can you limit your exposure to them?" If there's one person in your office that tends to be a downer, try and think of ways that you and your playmates can strike first—this is called the power lead, by the way. A power lead is simply influencing the direction of a conversation or interaction by beginning it with something positive. Like I've said before, emotions are contagious, so whatever emotion is present first will carry the tone of the entire interaction.

If there's even one individual that tends to show up all the time like, "Oh, woe is me, when do we leave?" That will be the vibe of the entire day! But if someone comes in, starting meetings with an icebreaker or an activity to get the room's energy up, or finding the wonder and joy around them, that play-like spirit will persist throughout the whole day. But you already know this, Play Rebel. I'm just trying to point out that if you look hard enough, have a little patience, and are honest with yourself, you can categorize the barriers you face. You'll find that most things that inhibit play will fall under one of three categories; How we think, how we feel, and our environment.

## #7 Recognizing Your Personal Barriers

Ok, Play Rebel, it's time to take a good look at your own barriers and begin formulating a plan of action! The first thing to do is to assess your state of mind and how you've been thinking. Where have your energy levels been lately? Think of your environment as well. Is there something that could be inhibiting play in your life right now? Use Maslow's hierarchy of needs and the questions I mentioned before, here they are again:

- O Are all my physiological needs met?
- O Do I feel safe?
- O Do I feel some sense of social belonging?
- O Do I feel respected and/or adequate?

Find out if there is something not right and what it might be. Then think of what sort of playful challenge you can do to fix the issue. Once you find out what you're missing or the need that isn't satisfied, you can playfully overcome your barriers with the information and tools you have and your playful spirit.

## #8 Name Your Guilt Exercise

Refusing to acknowledge your guilt might temporarily keep it from spilling into your everyday life, but masking your emotions won't work as a permanent strategy. Honestly addressing guilt requires you to first accept your feelings, however unpleasant they are.

Give this exercise a try:

1.    Set aside some quiet time for yourself.

2.    Bring along a journal to keep track of your thoughts.

3.    Say to yourself, or write down, what happened: "I feel guilty because I shouted at my kids." "I broke a promise." "I cheated on a test."

4.    Mentally open the door to guilt, frustration, regret, anger, and any other emotions that might come up. Writing down what you feel can help.

5.    Sit with those feelings and explore them with curiosity instead of judgment. Many situations are more complex than they first appear, and picking apart the knot of emotions can help you get a better handle on what you're really feeling.

THE PLAYREBEL
FIELD GUIDE

CHAPTER 9:

# THE PLAY REBEL FIELD GUIDE

# CHAPTER 9: THE PLAY REBEL FIELD GUIDE

Well, Play Rebel, you've made it to the end, and I'm so proud of you! I hope I've been able to help you recalibrate your Compass of Joy and find your way from the proving grounds to your playground. Once there, you'll be able to avoid burnout and become a joyful, playful rebel in our fun little revolution. We haven't decided on a handshake yet, but we do have a promise:

# The Playful Rebel Promise

Today I choose to be playful.

I choose to rebel against the status quo of work that says that play is a waste of time. No longer will I give up control in fulfilling my life's passions.

I will intentionally add playful moments that are designed to power me up and give me the ability to step into the powerful person that I know I am capable of being.

I have a challenge mindset; I get fired up when I think about tackling the obstacles in my life. I choose to celebrate my successes no matter how small they may be.

Each day I will invite myself to be curious and willing to observe the opportunities that life brings regardless of how I feel in the moment.

I will be mindful of my energy levels and follow my Compass of Joy to rejuvenate myself as needed.

I will seek out opportunities to play with others to return to our natural state of being: compassion, curiosity, and creativity.

I will do my best to make sure that I honor this Promise in every aspect of my day because I deserve it. I am worthy of it, I know play is normal, and it will help me be my most authentic self.

Because I choose to be playful, I am giving others permission to do the same.

## The Playful Virtues and Rebellious Actions

### Commitment to Joy

- ⭕ Find the fun in a mundane task
- ⭕ Do something that brings you joy

### Activate Power-Ups and Downs

- ⭕ Power up/down before/after a task
- ⭕ Celebrating tiny wins

### Radical Acceptance of Reality

### Reframe Your Failures

- ⭕ Practice "Yes, and…"

## ☆ Seek out Invitations to Play

- O   Get outside your comfort zone
- O   Turn disruption into an opportunity for play

## ☆ Creating a Moment of Connection with Someone

- O   Connections with playmates
- O   We > Me

Now celebrate your win in true Play Rebel fashion. To help you out, I've included some exercises to get you started. Use these if you're feeling a little stuck or for some inspiration to create your own playful activities.

**Exercise your imagination.** The next time you find yourself in a lobby, at a window, or just with an odd moment somewhere, take a look around yourself and try to remember how your five-year-old self would have seen your surroundings. Is that a dumpster or could it be a dragon? That noisy air conditioner in the doctor's office might just need repair, but your playful spirit might hear an evil robot sneaking down the hall!

## Power-Ups

**Keep a brag book.** Journal at least one thing every day that you're proud of.

**Borrow a victory.** Sometimes we have those days where it seems all the chips are down, and nothing can go right.

If your Brag Book is looking a little bare, go ahead and borrow one of these classic examples that people forget about all the time!

- Survived being born
- Survived my childhood
- Survived my child's childhood
- Learned to walk
- Ran a race
- Rode a bike
- Asked for help
- Faced a fear
- Did a chore
- Performed an act of kindness (*Bonus points if it was playful!)
- Forgave someone
- Learned to drive
- Learned something new
- Created something
- Taught something
- Spoke out

- O  Shared something
- O  Accepted love or friendship

**Ten Joyful Things Exercise.** This is a good one to add to your Brag Book, too. Wherever you are, take five minutes to write down ten things in your environment that you can feel joyful about. This not only gets your mind in a positive mindset but helps you get used to actively searching for fun and play.

**Challenge a friend** to a "Fake Laugh" contest. Whoever can come up with the most ridiculous laugh wins, although good luck trying to fake it!

## Tell your child/pet how awesome they are!

**Snap the pic** the next time you surprise yourself with the front-facing camera on your phone. Just go with it; if nothing else, you can save it to giggle at later.

## Power Downs

**Practice doing something wrong.** Draw a picture with your nondominant hand, make your bed with the pillows at the opposite end, or have dinner for breakfast just to find out how fun "mistakes" can be!

**Release your frustrations!** The next time you really see red, try doing an interpretive dance to show—at least to your mirror—how you really feel! Turn on some angry music and express yourself.

**Make a change!** No matter where you work—whether from home or a commute away—change out of your work clothes when you're done working. This gives your brain a cue to wind down.

**Rehearse a conversation** with a historical figure. Tell Babe Ruth how much you love the candy bar!

## Bonus Round

**Decide on your soundtrack.** Go ahead, Play Rebel; we all fantasize about being in the movies, so what would YOUR theme song be? Don't stop there either! Pick out some invigorating "chase" music for your morning commute, and maybe even something from your favorite caper flick for when you're doing the dishes or leaving a meeting!

**For our Play Rebels in business suits,** try putting on a temporary tattoo where it won't be seen, or go wild and dig out those whacky underwear from college to wear under your business casuals!

**Challenge a coworker/family member/ friendly stranger** to a paper tube duel. Next time you find yourself with a couple of convenient "weapons" of the playful variety, gallantly offer one to whoever happens to be nearest, they'll know what's up right away! (Just be sure to be respectful if they say no and move on to another playmate.)

**Use a balloon, nerf, or "paper football"** to pass the speaking privileges at your next meeting. Another variation is to use a crazy hat.

**Forget the suggestion box**, try putting up an Inspiration Box instead. Use it as a positivity boost for your office and ask people to put in their inspiring and positive comments —everything from "We're going to rock the bid on Friday!" to "Mike's doing an amazing job his first week; let's all welcome him."

# The world is your Playground, Rebel, so go forth, grab your playmates, and spread the joy!

We'd love to see you on the playground of life! Use the hashtag #playfulrebellion #permissionToPlay on social media, or join the community at breakthroughplay.com/rebellion

# Conclusion

Thank you for making it through to the end of Playful Rebellion: Maximize Workplace Success through the Power of Play. I hope your Compass of Joy is pointing to your playground, and you're showing all your playmates how to find theirs.

The next step is to keep play a priority and accept the invitations that the universe presents to you. Celebrate your wins vigorously, and failures even more so. And don't forget to rest and make new connections.

I appreciate you for being courageous and rebelling against the status quo and prioritizing play and playfulness. Your effort is going to give someone else permission to play too!
Finally, if you found this book useful in any way, a review on Amazon is always appreciated!

# Resources/Bibliography

Hook, Nick Castle- Director, Amblin Entertainment, December 11, 1991

The Sandlot, David Mickey Evans- Director, Island World, April 7, 1993

Ware, B (2012) The Top Five Regrets Of The Dying: A life transformed by the dearly departing. Hay House Inc. https://www.amazon.com/Top-Five-Regrets-Dying-Transformed/dp/140194065X

Brown, S (2010) Play: How it shapes the brain, opens the imagination, and invigorates the soul. Avery. https://doi.org/10.1177%2F1057083720940301

Brown, S (2014) Consequences Of Play Deprivation. Scolarpedia.org https://doi.org/10.4249/scholarpedia.30449

C.L. van den Berg, T. Hol, J. M. Van Ree, B.M. Sprujit, H. Everts, J. M. Koolhaas (1999) Play is indispensable for an adequate development of coping with social challenges in the rat. Dev. Psychobiol. 34, 129–138. https://doi.org/10.1002/(SICI)1098-2302(199903)34:2<129::AID-DEV6>3.0.CO;2-L

Anthony Veneziale is a leader in the field of improvisation and teaching, with over 25 years of improv performances around the globe. https://www.anthonydveneziale.com/

Gordon, G. Esbjörn-Hargens, S. (2007) Are We Having Fun Yet? an Exploration of the Transformative Power of Play https://doi.org/10.1177/0022167806297034

Fogg, B.J. (2020) Tiny Habits: The Small Changes That Change Everything. Houghton Mifflin Harcourt https://www.amazon.com/Tiny-Habits-Changes-Change-Everything/dp/0358003326

McGonigal, J. (2010) TED Talk https://janemcgonigal.com/2014/01/06/transcript-games-can-make-a-better-world/

Jane McGonigal: Gaming can make a better world | TED Talk .... https://www.ted.com/talks/jane_mcgonigal_gaming_can_make_a_better_world/transcript

McGonigal, J ( 2016) Superbetter: The Power Of Living Game fully. Penguin Books. https://www.amazon.com/Super Better-Living-Gamefully-Jane-McGonigal/dp/0143109774

Coach Dave Buck, CEO, Master Certified Coach and founding member of the Transformational Leadership Council. http://www.coachville.com/

Gilbert, E. (2015) Big Magic: Creative Living Beyond Fear. River head Books. https://www.amazon.com/Big-Magic-Creative-Living-Beyond/dp/1594634726

Pohler, M. (2021) The Hello, Fears Challenge: A 100-Day Journal for self-discovery. Sourcebooks. https://www.amazon.com/Hello-Fears-Challenge-100-Day-Self-Discovery/dp/1728234441

Van Edwards, V (2017) Captivate: The science of succeeding with people. Portfolio.

Tarvin, A (2019) Humor That Works: The missing skill for success and happiness at work. Where to study improv in Barcelona - ShBarcelona. https://www.shbarcelona.com/blog/en/improv/

Kashdan, T. (2009) Curious?: Discover the Missing Ingredient to a Fulfilling Life. William Morrow. https://www.amazon.com/Curious-Discover-Missing-Ingredient-Fulfilling/dp/0061661198 Resilience, mental health and the workplace | Leapfrog .... https://www.leapfrogjobs.com/article/resilience-mental-health-and-workplace

# Other Resources

TED 2017 Tim Ferriss - Why you should define your fears
   instead of your goals: https://www.ted.com/talks/tim_fer
   riss_why_you_should_define_your_fears_instead_of_
   your_goals?language=en

Young at Heart: A Perspective for Advancing Research
   on Play in Adulthood: https://journals.sagepub.com/doi/
   abs/10.1177/1745691615596789

Play at Work: An Integrative Review and Agenda for
   Future Research: https://journals.sagepub.com/doi/
   full/10.1177/0149206317731519

5 Ways To Bring Back : https://www.mayoclinic.org/tests-proce
   dures/resilience-training/in-depth/5-ways-to-bring-play-
   back-into-your-life/art-20342117

I Play At Work—Ten principles for transforming work processes
   through gamification: https://www.ncbi.nlm.nih.gov/
   pmc/articles/PMC3906598/

The Importance of Play - University of Cambridge: http://www.
importanceofplay.eu/IMG/pdf/dr_david_whitebread_-_
the_importance_of_play.pdf

Six reasons why fun in the office is the future of work - CIPHR:
https://www.ciphr.com/advice/fun-in-the-office/

Why it's good for grown-ups to go play: https://www.washington
post.com/national/health-science/why-its-good-for-
grown-ups-to-go-play/2017/05/19/99810292-fd1f-11e6-
8ebe-6e0dbe4f2bca_story.html

# Acknowledgements

To you! Thank you for selecting this book. Regardless of if you bought it, borrowed it, or it was given to you, I hope you got something that will help you embrace your inner Play Rebel.

To my wife, Courtney Ware. Thank you for supporting me down this crazy path called life. Your belief in me is what inspired me to double down on being a play facilitator, which ultimately led me to writing this book. Thank you for being my rock and partner. I love you.

To my parents, Lois and Garcia Ware, thank you for your support and instilling in me strong values and giving me the space to be curious and creative. I like to think that jumping off the roof with an umbrella and the holes in the wall were just practice to get me ready for a life of play.

To my sisters, Loicia and Leitacia Ware, thank you for putting up with all my Big Brother antics. You two are the best little sisters a guy could have.

To my playful colleagues Apryl, Jeff, Kirsten, Amy, Jan, Luis, Paul, and the rest of the Play and Ponder community. Thank you for the accountability and helping me pull this book through the finish line. I appreciate you!

To my mentors, specifically Gwen Gordon, Dave Buck, Michael Bernoff, Ryan Berman, and Tania Katan. Thank you for your wisdom and guidance over the years and for paving a path for me to follow. To Ryan and Tania, thank you for reviewing my manuscript and giving me feedback to take it to the next level. Though I did not take all the advice, just know that your effort did not go on deaf ears. I appreciate you for believing in me and inspiring me to have courage and to be a creative trespasser.

To my book collaboration team. To my campaign manager Hannah Stomski, if it wasn't for your hard work in helping me promote the book I think the only person that would have purchased it would have been my mom. To my book designer Bex Olesek, thank you for taking my manuscript and transforming it to a playful work of art. To my Illustrator Sarah Moyle, your illustrations are amazing and gave the book the POP I was looking for. Finally to my editor Cristi Cross, thank you for your playful approach to writing a book. If it wasn't for you this would still be a thought in my head. I appreciate you four amazing women greatly!

# About the Author

Gary Ware, the founder of Breakthrough Play, is a corporate facilitator, keynote speaker, certified coach, and self-proclaimed Creative Catalyst. Gary has over fourteen years of experience in the corporate world holding various leadership positions. Being a multifaceted individual, Gary also comes with nearly a decade of experience as a performer in improv theatre. After experiencing burnout in his pursuit for success and happiness, he realized that what was missing was play. Committing to a life of play is what led Gary to discover his passion for facilitating. Gary uses the power of applied improvisation and other playful methods to assist people in unlocking creativity, confidence, and better communication. Gary was recently featured as one of the Top 100 HR influencers of 2021 by the Engagedly HR software platform. When Gary isn't leading workshops or speaking, you can find him learning magic or off on an adventure with his wife, Courtney, and sons, Garrett and Cameron.

If you would like to use the power of play to activate your team or event, Gary is available for workshops and talks. You can find more information at breakthroughplay.com/training.

# About the Illustrator

Sarah Moyle, Creative Catalyst and Visual Storyteller, is a creative facilitator, speaker, and illustrator. Since creating her own unique role at Intel Corporation shortly after joining the company in 2011, Sarah has been a champion of play, creativity, and visual thinking at Intel and beyond. She is passionate about reigniting and fostering the inate creativity and playfulness in everyone she works with to have hard fun and unlock innovative ideas. When she isn't playing at Intel, Sarah delights in getting outdoors with her son, Owen, and daughter Mila, crafting, and making spooky plans for her elaborate Halloween display each year!